Radio Nowhere 2008

Thoughts, Rough Drafts and Letters Home

A LiveJournal Blog

Written by Mark Stratton
Introduction by Van Reid

All contents Copyright © 2008-2009 Mark Stratton except:

Introduction Copyright © 2009 Van Reid
"Good for Goose, Good for Gander" (Guest Post, 10/18/08)
Copyright © 2008 Van Reid
Dibbles Illustration 2008 © Copyright Mike Worley

Front Cover drawn by Bruce Rosenberger, colored by Randy Sargent, 2009 © Copyright Bruce Rosenberger

Used with Permission

For Elaine

Preface

I started <u>Radio Nowhere</u> as more of a lark than anything else. No real reason other than I wanted to 'write stuff.' In that I have succeeded admirably. I 'wrote stuff.' Some was good, some wasn't and some was about what you'd expect on the Internet.

In some ways, some of the posts I wrote were along the lines of a half sauced man in a tavern spouting off to anyone who would listen. Others, fairly well thought out and decently written. And a few were just plain goofy. Which is okay. Life without some goofy in it is hardly worth living.

I swear, I bloviate, I pontificate, I politic, I screed, I poem, I remember and I 'write stuff' that I felt needed to be written. For no other audience than myself at times.

I had originally intended on having the comments Radio Nowhere generated included. They add a real flavor and sense of life or community to many of the entries. However, for reasons that have more to do with copyright than anything else, I elected not to.

The comments can be found on <u>Radio Nowhere</u> (htp://ying-ko-4.livejournal.com) and you are more than welcome to check them out.

I want to thank everyone who has taken time to read what I wrote, commented on what I wrote or encouraged me to keep writing. It's been fun and the journey continues.

Mark Stratton
July 2009

He's on the Road to Somewhere
(On Radio Nowhere)

I can picture him on his Gold Wing (that's a motorcycle; and sure, I had to learn that, too), schooling down the highway in search of a good ball game (Cardinals preferred), humming something from an obscure Al Stewart album (Does he listen to his iPod while driving that thing?), and more or less secure in the knowledge that he has a good book and a couple of comics in his saddlebags. With no more warning then you ever get in these situations, somebody in an SUV, driving too fast and with a cell-phone sticking out of their ear canal, doesn't even realize that they've cut him off. The Gold Winger is royally frosted because, you know, there is just no excuse for bad manners!!!! He's already considering the wording on Radio Nowhere.

But, as it happens, it's not only bad manners that come without warning. When he stops at the next light, a family is crossing the street and a little kid turns toward the motorcycle (and, more importantly, toward the motorcyclist) and waves with a smile.

Guess which incident he's taking home to Elaine, because what he's really secure about, what it all pretty much wraps around is the person who will be home when he comes back. He speaks of her (well, writes of her) with such respect and devotion that I want to meet her as much as I want to meet him, and I've never exchanged a word with her.

Both instances will be broadcast, but the little kid will get the spotlight. Yeah, I made it all up, but that's how I imagine him. We've never met, as you will have guessed – not in the real world.

The internet is a wilderness in the truest sense of the word. It's wild out there. There are groves and thickets, trustworthy deer paths and treacherous swamps. There is no single voice in the wilderness. There's a skinny-zillion of them and at least one behind every virtual tree. It's a cacophony of voices in the wilderness and it takes some learning and experience to know which ones to filter out and which ones to tune in. You triangulate those that become important to you. I'm scanning the internet waves – a neophyte - and here's someone who lives music, likes western stories in print and on film, and reads comics! I begin to pinpoint where he roams. He's a baseball fan! He's got a code he lives by, but he's not rigid with it. I fine tune the radio, because this is a voice I don't want to lose. One day, while in an internet discussion that has become unexpectedly distressing and when I find myself the subject of an upsetting (to my naïve sensibilities) verbal attack, the Gold Winger's voice cruises out of the wilderness and has my back, expressing the outrage of a friend I didn't know I had. The Kid from Missouri smiles and waves as he takes the crosswalk.

Guess which incident I take home with me!

It won't be the last time. And, in a way, the best thing about it is that the Gold Winger and I don't always agree about music and baseball and comics or whatever. And it doesn't matter; there's a mutual respect for differing ideas. Who better to have your back than someone who is not facing the exact same direction?

But then, over the next months and – yes - years, something else happens with amazing regularity: He makes me laugh out loud as much as any other voice in these woods. And, you know, Uncle John always said that a sense of humor is the surest sign of intelligence. And, you know, making someone laugh out loud with the printed word is not necessarily an easy thing to do. He just makes it seem easy.

I'm just saying.

We've never met in the real world. I've never shaken his hand. I haven't got a perfect fix on those Missourian wilds he cycles through (heck, I haven't got a perfect fix on my own Maine wilderness), but I'm triangulating or septangulating or something like that. Sometimes the roar of the Gold Wing is part of the voice and the voice comes through clear over the engine. Sometimes the Missouri Kid waves and you can hear the voice clear with the gesture and the smile.

He calls this Radio Nowhere. I say, that's a joke, son. He's on the Road to Somewhere on his Radio Nowhere, cruising his Gold Wing on curiosity and thought, talking music and baseball and literature and what have you – a lot of what have you. He writes poetry. It's all worth the airtime because what it all boils down to is good company and a sincere voice in the thickets and swamps of the internet wilds.

And, here, you don't even have to brave them.

Moxie!

Van Reid
Edgecomb, ME
February, 2009

What Do You Have To Say? -My Guilty Pleasure

(2008-01-03 11:27)

LJ Question: What's your guilty pleasure?

I have two I'm not crazy about admitting to. Especially in public. Since nobody reads this, what the hell...

- Neil Diamond would be the musical guilty pleasure. I know that way back in the '60's he could rock your AM radio to pieces, and do it well, he fell into psuedo Vegas schlockdom in the mid-70's. And he's mined that particular area fairly well ever since. Still, there's a nauseatingly endearing quality to such treacle as "Hello, Again" and "Forever in Blue Jeans" and "Heartlight" that's hard to deny or ignore.
- The Waltons TV show is equally treacly in places, and for poor folks, they had a lot of house and other things. Granted, it was a tough time and all, but it still seemed a bit far-fetched at times. In the beginning of the series, Olivia wasn't at all a sympathetic character, although she did grow as the series progressed. At least when she was on the show, that is. Still, it gave me a look at a family dynamic that wasn't present in my home, that I desperately wanted to have. It still brings back warm feelings of fleeting times of well-being and comfort from my younger days.

What's been going on, you ask? (2008-01-03 13:09)

This blog was originally started for a simple reason, one which is no longer relevant. Truth be told, I almost forgot it was around. Sad, huh? I think so.

I had wanted to get back to some sort of regular blogging/journaling/diary/whatever you want to call it, but family pressures interfered. The demands on my time as my Grandmother was dying were too much for me to actually think about any online writing, nor did I do any real world writing to speak of. After Grandma passed, a spiral of depression followed and I did little of any creative nature or worth in the time after that. Which is a shame as I did some fairly interesting (to me, at least) and fun things. Pity that I didn't write about my trip to L.A. to visit Brian or heading to San Diego from there with Eddie. Or our three trips to Ohio to visit family or heading to Chicago to visit friends from California who were traveling there.

There's also the purchase of two motorcycles this past year and some trips around the state, and the celebration of 9 years of marriage to my wonderful wife, watching our dear friends pass the 30 year milestone of wedded bliss and watching the nieces and nephews get older.

As the depression recedes (thanks to medication), I feel the need to write again. It's almost a compulsion, to be honest. As I was looking at the Livejournal site, trying to reacquaint myself with things, I saw the question about guilty pleasures. I decided to answer that as a writing exercise and to flex some of those unused skills. Already, I see things I would've done differently.

I guess nobody is ever satisfied with their writing, are they?

What Do You Have To Say? -Ten Years From Now... (2008-01-04 14:23)

LJ Question: Where do you think you'll be in ten years?

I don't know where I'll actually be, but I'd still like to be married to my wife. I don't see why that won't happen as we get along very well, and I truly think she's a lovely and wonderful woman. God forbid that she'd get tired of me or something... The other thing I'd like to see happen is an improvement in the relationship with my daughter, which would bring me great joy.

First Ride of 2008 (2008-01-05 21:31)

The temperature has been a bit on the chilly side for riding a motorcycle. Although, I do have to admit to a certain admiration for the poor slobs who appear to have little choice but to ride those little scooters during this time of year, for me it's been too cold to ride my motorcycles. Today, the weather finally cooperated, and I pulled the Suzuki Boulevard C-50 out of the garage and got it ready for the first ride of this young year, and the first ride I've taken on it since sometime in November. After getting all ready, which means leather jacket with a Thinsulate liner, gloves, full face helmet and a tank of gas (plus other boring stuff like checking the tires and stuff), I set out for a short ride before meeting my wife at the local Chuck E Cheese noisateria for a birthday party for our niece who turned a year old. After those festivities, and some visiting, I headed out for a trip through the northern part of Boone County. Some nice roads in the area, and not heavily trafficked made for a nice ride. The temperature was in the mid 50's, which is nice riding weather, and the roads were mostly dry, yet there were plenty of spots of wetness. Mostly, it's the same thing that happens whenever the temperature goes up after a prolonged period of cold. I'm not sure why that is, but I know that is just is. The phenomenon was more pronounced in shaded areas, which should come as no surprise to anyone at all. This made a few places a bit slick, or gave the appearance of that anyhow. A bit of caution and I just went along my way. I like riding with others, and I especially like having my wife along for the ride, but when I do venture off by myself, I find it enjoyable. I like the chance to clear my head, not let the radio or iPod get my attention and with the part of my brain that isn't working trying to keep me alive avoiding things like idiot drivers, deer, potholes, sharp turns or curves, I wander over the landscape of my life, think about things and clear my head. Even a short ride of 40-50 miles can be therapeutic. There were some signs of the season still around, such as large areas of ice on ponds despite the increase in temperatures, as well as ice in creeks. Kind of an odd contrast as I tend to associate riding with warmer weather. Still, it's great to be able to ride in the middle of winter. One of the upsides to living in Missouri, I guess. I didn't go anywhere really special, nor did I see anything of great note. Still, for all that, it was a great day to be out on two wheels, and tomorrow is supposed to be even warmer. Elaine is actually considering going with me for a ride, which would be marvelous.

Nicole Atkins (2008-01-06 20:38)

October 30, 2006 was the release date of Nicole Atkins debut CD, Neptune City. I'd been looking forward to this for some time, and having suffered through a delay of the original ship date, I was ecstatic that it has finally arrived in stores. She celebrated by performing on the Letterman Show with a stunning rendition of "The Way It Is" to marvelous effect.

I've no idea how I actually first stumbled across Atkins or her music. I do know that when I did, I was hooked. I do recall the first song was an mp3 download from some web site of "The Way it Is" and that it rapidly became one of the most listened to songs on my Last.fm playlist. The Orbison-esque sound of the song, with the addition of that Wall of Sound so evocative of Phil Spector captivated me. I found a couple of other songs around the internet, then bought a copy of her already out of print EP "Bleeding Diamonds." This was amazing, heady stuff I was listening to. I looked at my Last.fm charts and soon had almost 200 plays of Nicole Atkins. This is a nifty trick with all of 8 songs to choose from. I landed an advance copy of "Neptune City" and was enraptured. This was scintillating music. There is a sense of melancholy in the title track as she reminisces about her hometown (Neptune City, NJ) and the changes that occur over time. The video for the song, released long before the album, works to tell this story. Great stuff...

Atkins uses words and music to paint sweeping images and feelings. There's a hint of David Lynch to her work, and it's apparent that she has listened to and flavored her music with a history of musical sound. Neptune City is a terrific album and one I recommend you to at least give a listen to. There are a few songs for listening on her Myspace page, tour information and news on her web site and there's more videos on her very own Youtube page.

Acquaintances (2008-01-07 09:17)

When we were at our niece's birthday party, we saw people we don't see very often. Not that we don't like them, but as you get older, keeping in closer touch with every person you know becomes increasingly difficult. Sometimes, news doesn't filter out to acquaintances and can occasionally create an awkward situation. Like the one that occurred Saturday.

Alyssa used to work with my wife, and has since moved on to other pursuits. She married a friend of our niece's father, hence her presence at the noisateria that is Chuck E. Cheese's (which was easily as loud as the Shiny Toy Guns concert I went to last fall). She asked my how my grandmother was, and I was sort of struck by the question. She passed away last February and I hadn't had anyone ask that in a while. I was pleased she was interested, but had to tell her she passed away almost a year ago. Her face fell almost down to her shoes in shock. Apparently, she'd no idea this had happened and she felt awful. Awful for not knowing, and awful for apparently making a social faux pas. Which was not big deal to me, as it never occurred to me that she would or wouldn't know. I honestly never thought about it.
Anyway, it was an interesting social moment and it just sort of made me think a bit.

What Do You Have To Say? -My Favorite Shot (2008-01-07 10:30)

LJ Question: Describe your favorite photograph.

For me, it would have to be a photo taken of my maternal Grandfather on the bridge of a cruise ship. There he stands, with a captain's hat jauntily positioned on his head, with a small smile. What struck me then, and still does, it the look of relaxation. Granddad seldom relaxed and I believe it was one of those things he never quite learned to do well. He'd worked since he was around 7 years old, and if he wasn't working, he was thinking about working, or worrying over something. Relaxing seemed to be a foriegn concept to him. Except in this one photograph. I don't know if it's my favorite photograph, but it does belong in the top 10, at least.

What Do You Have To Say? -To Shoot or Be Shot? (2008-01-08 11:22)

LJ Question: Do you like being behind the camera or in front of the camera?

Oh hell, that's easy. I'm just a big fat tub of goo, so hand me the camera and let me take your picture. Of course, that could change in a years time...

What Do You Have To Say? -I Spy... (2008-01-13 22:29)

LJ Question: Look around. Describe the first photograph you see. What does it mean to you?

It is a large poster-sized print of the Katy Railroad, taken by Bob Lindhom, not long before the rail line was abandoned and converted to a State Park. It was taken from the bluffs overlooking the rail line along the Missouri River west of Columbia, MO with the Missouri River Bridge crossing the river. It is a treasured gift from some very dear friends. They gave it to me for Christmas, back in 1987. It has held a place of honor in every place I've lived since then. It's been a source of comfort and more than a token of the season. It was and remains a source of inspiration and the value of friendship. These same friends spent this past Christmas with us and will always be welcome. They are friends we choose to call family.

What Do You Have To Say? -Put It On Repeat (2008-01-14 09:55)

LJ Question: If you could only listen to one album for the rest of your life, which one would it be (and why)?

Bruce Springsteen's "Born to Run" is the perfect album from start to finish. But, since I like a lot of variety, even it would wear out after a time. This is a nigh impossible question to answer, when you get right down to it. AUGH!

What Do You Have To Say? -The Soundtrack of My Life (2008-01-16 19:56)

LJ Question: What songs would you include on the "soundtrack of your life?"

That's such a hard question. Not because I can't think of any great songs that have personal meaning or bring back evocative feelings, it's mainly because it's such a fluid thing. It changes, like I do, over the years. I guess you could look at my [1]Last.fm profile and get a sense of what I've been listening to over the past 18 months or so, but it's not representative of the soundtrack of my life. I have [2]a list of albums that fall under that category, and I am much more of an album listener than a singles listener. Have been for donkey's years, I guess. That old AOR radio coming back to bite me, I suppose. Still, even that album list is hardly what I listen to a lot these days. They are old, dear friends and when I listen to them, it's like a reunion with a past self or time. That, or I play it loud as hell...(LOL!)

1. http://www.last.fm/user/Big_Baby_Jesus
2. http://rateyourmusic.com/list/Big_Baby_Jesus/soundtrack_of_my_life

Trip to the Dentist (2008-01-16 20:39)

I got to experience that rare joy of going to the dentist. Not something most of us look forward to, but something quite a lot of us do. As dentists go, he's not a bad guy. Passionate about dentistry, which can be a good thing. I do remember him telling me once that he knew when he was about 12 that he knew he wanted to be a dentist. An odd occupation choice at that age, but what the hell...

Getting a tooth drilled, whilst having a rubber dam clamped in your mouth is not my idea of fun. Watching paint dry while listening to the Best of Tiffany, being played at ear drum shattering volume and being trussed up in a straightjacket is roughly the same level of torment as this. However, there was a large area of yucky that the good dentist determined needed to be taken away, and away it has been taken. I know have a temporary crown, and get a permanent one next month.

Great news and I'll bet your wondering why the hell I mentioned this, right?

Here's the scoop...I got to thinking that we tend to place a lot of trust in people we barely know to do certain jobs, yet have a hard time trusting people we know much better in smaller matters. Which is a conundrum I find interesting. No rational reason comes to mind, but it's also indicative of how far the mind wanders when there is the lovely aroma of over-heated tooth enamel and latex from the rubber dam circulating in the air. That, and the knowledge there's some guy shoving needles and a drill in your mouth...

I also got to wondering whatever happened to Marathon Bars...

This thing called writing... (2008-01-17 13:47)

This thing called writing can be fun, or it can be irritating or daunting or whatever you want it to be. Or whatever it turns out to be to you or appears or morphs into. Sometimes things come easy, sometimes the paper/screen mock you as you attempt to fill in the space or regurgitate words or thoughts or ramblings or musings or recipes. Or whatever is spinning round in your head/heart at that given moment.

Do you write on paper or on-line only? A journal that will survive the server crash that only one at a time can read? Do you write in both forms? Is it a compulsion or a flight of fancy?

What is this thing called writing?

And He Cries... (2008-01-17 16:12)

On a Winter's Day
Texas Stadium
Romo Gets Picked
The Clock Winds Down
And T.O. Cries

Passes Dropped Like Flies
America's Team
Swatted by Giants
The Post Game Show
And T.O. Cries

Don't Blame Jessica
Says the Receiver
That's So Unfair
That's My Q.B!
And T.O. Cries...

The Soundtrack of My Life (2008-01-20 13:38)

There was a question not long ago concerning what songs would you put on the soundtrack of your life. While I thought it was an interesting question, I considered it some and came to the conclusion that it was fairly limiting as there is so much more to the sounds of a life than music. As I thought about this some more, I hauled out my Moleskine and wrote these down. They follow in no particular order or importance, as they are all important to me.

- My Mother's voice, silent now.
- "Sunday, Monday, Happy Days..."
- My daughter's first cry
- Three women who said, "I do," the two who don't, and the One who always will
- Crickets
- Ernie Harwell when I was a boy
- Jack Buck as I grew older
- "New York, New York" as the last dance
- **Mrs. Tarantino:** Are you the police? **Elwood:** No, ma'am. We're musicians.
- "Stop picking on your sister" and I wish I had
- Barking dogs
- Concert Band in Jr. High School
- Songs I've song and Songs I've heard
- Shooting baskets
- bicycle tires on pavement
- autumn leaves, rustling in the breeze
- Thunderstorms
- The last day of school
- Church Hymns
- Phones ringing
- WCCO/WJR/WAAM/CKLW/WRIF/WDRQ/WLLZ/WAPL/WIXX/WNFL/KFMZ/KCMQ/WLS/KBIA/KFRU/BXR/KTGR/ Jack FM
- J.P. McCarthy
- CBS Radio Mystery Theater
- Jimmy Launce and Hortense Waffle Day
- "Due to snow, the following schools are closed..."
- My daughter saying, "Daddy, I love you" (Not heard in some time)
- "This is a test, this is only a test..."
- "President Reagen has been shot."
- The Star-Spangled Banner
- "Party on the Hill tonight!"

- "Honey! You're Home!"
- My wife's laughter, and sadly her tears as well
- American Top 40 with [26]Casey Kasem
- Scooby-dooby Doo!
- The whispering voices of friends and others who have drifted into and out of my life
- "Spider-Man, Spider-Man, does whatever a spider can..."
- My Wife's smile

This list is hardly complete. I doubt it ever could be, to be truthful. It could become an ongoing thing, but most likely won't. Anyhow, it's just a smattering of things that have resonated with me, for one reason or another...There are a lot of stories here. Some will be told, and some others may not. These are sounds and noises and such that affected me over my life. Sounds that informed me, entertained me, amused me or made me cry. They are universal, yet uniquely mine. Hence, they make up a part of the soundtrack of my life. I had a hard time getting used to my summers without Jack Buck on my radio, and that still pops in my head when thinking about the sounds of summer in my life. That's why the contents of the soundtrack aren't constant, but always in a state of flux or growing as this journey of life keeps moving forward.

What Do You Have To Say? -The Last Time I Sang... (2008-01-20 17:18)

LJ Question: When was the last time you sang?

I sing in the car all the time. I found myself doing that on the Gold Wing as well, which could be very embarrassing if somebody actually heard me straining to hit the high notes of some song by Styx. (shudder) The last time I sang in public was for my Father-in-law's funeral. He asked me, shortly before he died, if I would do that for him. I was so touched and honored. I really loved the guy, so it was easy to say yes, but hard to actually do when the day came. Still, I made it through with only a small hiccup. The song? The old hymn, "In the Garden" was what he requested.

What Do You Have To Say? -When I Grow Up... (2008-01-22 10:10)

LJ Question: What do you want to be when you "grow up?"

I'm already grown up. I'd like to be less so. More in touch with my inner child and regain that sense of wonder of the world around me. I'd also like to be able to see my feet without leaning forward again.

(2008-01-22 17:46:18) I guess I'm technically grown up but I still feel like a little kid. :) Sometimes it's hard to find that middle ground where you're still seeing the world freshly & at the same time, you feel secure & independent. Jade

What Do You Have To Say? -Inspiring (2008-01-23 09:34)

LJ Question: What inspires you to create?

Sometimes it's something simple, like a chance comment or question. It gets me to thinking and the answers or thoughts gush and flow, then coalesce into something that makes sense to me. Other times it can come from something I read or watch on television and my mind wanders and the juices start flowing again. Typically with questions that are preceded with, "What if..." and away we go.

This message was approved by... (2008-01-23 20:49)

I get that candidates would want to make sure that they don't get misrepresented in campaign ads. If I were running for office, I sure wouldn't want some knothead group of political whacko's to endorse me and create ads that appear to have my approval. Talk about causing serious problems for an overly image conscious American public.

However, when I see ads that are done by the candidate them self, to have them tell me that they approve this message, after they've already given me the message, is kind of stupid on their part. It appears that they don't think we the electorate have sense enough to figure out that they mean what they say. There's also the possibility that they don't believe the electorate isn't smart enough to be aware of the fact that in order for them to have done their own campaign ad, they'd have to approve the darn thing in the first place.

So, how about instead of telling me, Joe Voter, that you approve what you just said, how about asking me for my vote instead? I remember that Tip O'Neill wrote in his book, Man of the House how important it was to ask for a vote, rather than presume that somebody will because they like you. I guess it's just the polite thing to do.

Writing on Paper (2008-01-24 17:42)

I love to write on paper. There's an amazing feeling that goes into putting pen to paper, and watch the blank page disappear and the words turn into phrases, then into sentences and paragraphs and soon you have a stream of thought, saved for posterity. Unless you happen to trash it, and start over. :o)

I've mentioned before that I keep a journal. I've used a couple of different journals/notebooks, and I've come to find that Apica CD-15 notebooks to be the one I like best. Since I use a fountain pen for almost all of my writing, I like the way the ink doesn't bleed through the page, and the paper works well with fountain pen tips and inks.

I also carry around with a Moleskine notebook. I have to admit, I'd never heard of one until a few years ago, and when I read the advertising propaganda about famous artists and the travel writer, I knew I had to have one. I figured that some creative juices would fall on my pen and there would be masterpiece after masterpiece gracing the pages. Sadly, there's pathetic poetry, scribbled notes and thoughts that seldom develop beyond their original appearance and die aborning. I have filled 2 of these little books, and they both have been taped up because I carry them almost everywhere I go. I'm currently on my third and they are wonderful little books to write in. Again, they work well with fountain pens, or at least the ones I use and that's all that's really important to me.

I derive true pleasure from writing with a fountain pen. The peaceful, friendly and comforting "scritch, scritch, scritch" that is made during writing is a marvelous thing. Much more tranquil than the clatter of keys being struck. That tactile sense of writing with a fountain pen, that nib with the ink flowing and creating something that can only be created by a fountain pen is quite a feeling. It's permanent. There is no delete key. You get it right the first time or your paper is filled with blots from scratching out your words. (That, or you just use it as a first draft and head for the computer when finished...lol!)

I have several fountain pens, and the one I've had the longest is a Rotring Core Fountain Pen. It's gone all over the country with me, and is quite dependable. I have a couple of hand made wooden barreled pens that were bought at craft fairs. They have great kit parts, and are quite attractive. I also have a Parker "51" that belonged to my Grandfather. I had it cleaned up, but have yet to use it. In fact, it may be some time before I use it. Mainly because I can't quite figure out how to fill the darn thing...

I sort of feel sorry for whoever gets stuck dealing with the journals. There's a lot of scribbles and hard to read material there. In recent years, I've taken to sticking things inside like comic strips clipped from the paper, or other such things. Hopefully, many years pass before this becomes a real worry...

There and Back Again...Sort of... (2008-01-26 19:21)

The day dawned bleak and gloomy. Gray overcast skies caused me to roll over and sleep a bit more. As the morning progressed, the clouds scudded to the east, leaving behind a glorious blue sky. The icy grip of winter was being relaxed for a couple of days, and I figured it was time to make hay while the sun was shining.

I started rummaging around, getting the leather jacket out, boots on and heading for the garage. I rolled the Gold Wing 1500 out and proceeded to start it up. Turned out, it was a non-starter. So much so, that I killed the battery in the attempt. So, back into the garage it went, and out came the Suzuki. That one fired right up, and I left it to idle for a few minutes and warm up. I grabbed my camera, notebook, cell phone and headed out for a ride. As the temperature was around 50 or so, it wasn't ideal, but it was wonderful to be out on two wheels.

I've been riding around two lane county highways across the county since I bought the C50 last spring, and I was looking for new roads to explore. Sadly, every one I started down turned into gravel before I'd gone very far. So, it was turn around and go back the way I came. Which was still traveling on two wheels on a winter's day. That was still a good thing.

However, I learned something. Never underestimate the power of a stout pair of socks. I was reminded of this in a theoretical sense, as I crossed small bridge and saw some this in a practical sense when my feet started getting very cold because I wasn't wearing solid enough socks under my boots! So, after 25 miles, I headed home and some heat.

It was great riding, even coping with the winter still in the air. There is something different about 50 degrees after days of below freezing temperatures and 50 degrees as you are heading into winter. I don't know how to explain it, but there it is. I was also pleased to see a couple of other riders out enjoying the rare winter treat.

Longer Ride (2008-01-27 20:04)

After I killed the battery on the Gold Wing, I decided I needed to go to Sears and buy a small battery charger, which I did. After running the charger all night, and rolling it out, I decided to slow down the process this time. After setting the choke, I flipped the throttle three times, let it rest a moment, then hit the starter. It fired right up the first time. I left the bike running, as it really needs to warm up a bit. It's a bit on the cold natured side, so I just have to coddle it a bit.

I got my boots on (good socks this time), rounded up the usual bike stuff, and headed out. I got a bit of gas, put a cassette adapter in the player (whoever thought of a tape player on a motorcycle was onto something), hooked up the iPod to it, selected an episode of CBS Radio Mystery Theater, and headed North. I went in a big circle, but I don't care. As the old show played itself out, I rolled on down the road. I stopped, created a playlist on the go, and headed along with the Marshall Tucker Band blaring from the speakers. It was pretty exhilarating, to be honest. For the most part, I stayed on fairly straight roads, but ended by riding back towards town by riding one of my favorite roads between Fulton and Columbia. It's a nice road to ride on a motorcycle, but I sometimes get swept away by memories.

Like the time I was heading to class at MU when I was living in Fulton, and there was a house on fire. I saw the owner running around with a garden hose trying to put it out, and stopped to help. Sadly, his house burned completely and all he saved were the family photo albums. That seemed to be the most important thing to him, so for that I was glad for him.

I also remember a mad drive at 1:30 in the morning or so on an April morning driving my ex-wife to the hospital so she could deliver our baby. It was a wild ride in a 1988 Festiva at a speed probably much higher than it was made to handle. I'm still not sure what was alarming my ex-wife more at the time; my driving or the labor pains. Or that I would just fall apart like the dithering idiot I was on the threshold of becoming.

I also remember the first time I rode that road when I got my first bike years ago. And how I was going to fast in one of the curves and would have ended up off the road if I hadn't come to an almost complete stop. Fortunately, there was nobody behind me and the only thing hurt was my nerves. It was an object lesson in not going too fast into curves. One I've kept in mind every time I hit that stretch.

I saw a few things that made me smile while I was riding today. Kids out throwing a football around, an old man burning leaves, a little girl walking with her father, birds on the wing, clear sky, familiar places, and some new ones as well. I rode down many familiar paths today, and saw many changes. I guess that reflects life in us all. Things may appear to stay the same, but they change and grow.

What Do You Have To Say? -I Made It Myself (2008-01-28 14:32)

LJ Question: What have you made using your own two hands?

I made a bowl out of clay for my mother when I was in the 6th grade. I painted (quite poorly) the same design as Captain America's shield on the inside of the bowl. I've not a blue clue in the world what happened to it since she died. I don't guess that building furniture that came in a box counts for much does it

Frank (2008-01-28 22:52)

I was listening to music recently (something I do quite a lot), and the old Charlie Daniels song, "The Devil Went Down to Georgia" came up on my iTunes. With over 10k songs, that's hardly surprising. What is surprising is the memories that came flooding back. Mainly, it made me think of the last time I went to Frank's house when I was in Green Bay visiting family.

I'd met Frank when I was attending De Pere High School. I had just moved there, and had some difficulty settling in. By the time I'd managed to give myself a less than stellar reputation, I couldn't be too choosy about who my friends were. Which really does Frank a disservice, as he wasn't a bad guy. Strange, to be sure. But, considering all that life had handed him up to that point, that made sense to me.

Frank had severe scoliosis. Long before I met him, when he was a boy, he had his back fused. Apparently, he was told he'd never walk, much less run. He did manage to walk, and run after a fashion. But, he had a pronounced hitch in his gitalong, and kids being kids (read: cruel), he was hung with the nickname, "Bun Bun." Why? I have no bloody idea, but there it is and there it was. Needless to say, he didn't like it very much. Which made calling him that mandatory, when the time was right. Like, when he was hitting on a girl.

Guys being guys, we tagged him with another nickname (Needledick), and we called him that whenever the embarrassment opportunity was highest. Like, you guessed it, when he was hitting on a girl. Which he did with alarming frequency. He could be charming as hell, and a lot of fun to bullshit with. However, he was just "different" enough that kids being kids, he was always the friend and seldom the boyfriend. Didn't keep him from trying, and I have to give him credit for that.

Frank was one of the most annoying, irritating, oddly compelling friends I ever had. He thought nothing of calling people at 2 in the morning if he couldn't sleep, which was far more often than the rest of us, apparently. I had to tell him in no uncertain terms not to do that. Mainly because I was drunk and was trying to pass out. Talking to somebody whilst trying to do that was difficult, to say the least.

Frank developed a love for cars and working on them. Never mind his physical limitations, he was bound and determined to learn to fix cars. He helped me to repair the 1966 Dodge Dart I'd bought when I was 17. Car wouldn't start, and had a lot of problems, but I'd dropped the whopping $75 on it, and I was going to see it running, and then drive it. After looking at a generic "How to fix your car" for complete idiots book, and a Chilton's manual for the specific car, we finally figured out that the Alternator was shot, and the voltage regulator was also no good. As a result, the battery was deader than a tax increase bill on a Republican's desk. So, after replacing said no good parts, the car fired right up. Ran like bloody hell, but it did run.

After that victory (a great moment in my life, I can assure you), we proceeded to do the things needed to tune the car up. Again, neither of us had any real knowledge about how to fix cars, but I guess I took my Dad's words (If you can read, you can fix most anything) to heart. Long story short, we got the car running pretty well for an old clunker.

After this, Frank started puttering around on cars, and then went to school to become a mechanic. He did well in school, but couldn't get a job because people were afraid he couldn't do the physical parts of the job. I guess it was a valid concern, but I'd love to have seen him try his hand at regardless.

Life had dealt Frank some nasty knocks. It saved the worst for last. Frank developed cancer. I don't really remember where it was, and it doesn't make any difference. It took his life. I had no idea that this had happened when I rang the bell at his folk's house. His mother answered the door and invited me in. We talked for awhile, and I asked about Frank. I thought she was going to stop breathing then and there.

She looked at me and said, "You don't know, do you?"

I must have looked about as dumb as a stump, because she continued with words that hammered into my head, "Buddy died 5 months ago..." (Buddy was his family nickname. He'd been named after his father...)

I asked some questions, we both sniffled and sobbed some. Then came the awkward silence because I had no idea what to say next. Frank's mom decided I needed something to remember him by, so she went to his room and brought down a Charlie Daniels record, <u>Million Mile Reflections</u> and gave it to me. That was 20 years ago. I didn't listen to it much, as it wasn't a great album. However, it had personal value to me, so I kept it for many years. I no longer have that album, as I unloaded all my vinyl a few years ago. Still, I have my memories of Frank and the time we were friends.

R.I.P. Frankie...

What Do You Have To Say? -Could Have Been Better
(2008-01-30 14:37)

**LJ Question: What's the worst thing you've ever made?
How could you have improved upon it?**

I wrote this short story years ago about a woman figuring out that her beloved mother had used her father, who everyone thought had abandoned the family, as fertilizer for her award winning tomatoes. It was one of those things that really seemed like a good idea at the time.

How would I make it better? Put that idea back and try something else. That's how...

There are days... (2008-01-30 16:25)

There are days when I sit down to write and this is all I get. It doesn't matter if I'm wanting to expound on the latest batch of navel lint I discovered, writing in my journal, a letter, or here. Sometimes, all I get is the big zilch. That, or I am totally unhappy with what I come up with. Or...don't like the reflection that I see.

Feel Like!! (2008-01-31 15:54)

There are songs that just leap out and grab me the very first time I hear them. Some, not all, prompt that same reaction every time I hear them, no matter how many times I listen to them. Al Stewart's "Feel Like" is one such song. It's the first track from his "Famous Last Words" album (and he's looking at a comic book on the cover!), and it really sets the tone for the album as a whole with it's driving acoustic guitar intro and strident rhythm.

> *I feel as volatile as the weather*
> *Over fields of Scottish heather*
> *The night before Halloween*
> *You know I feel like A catamaran in summer*
> *The beat of a reggae drummer*
> *The flag of a brigantine*

That first verse, coupled with the music, blends such pleasure and joy of life. It fairly crackles out of the speakers with vibrancy.

> *This is the day when*
> *All of my dreams came true*
> *This is the day when*
> *All of my life till now*
> *Seemed oh so blue*

Just a hint of the why of such happiness in the first half of the chorus.

> *You know I feel like A plate of the earth in motion*
> *A storm on the Indian Ocean*
> *A shake of a tambourine*

From major events to barely a whisper, from a perspective point of view I mean, what a great range of analogy here. Marvelous stuff.

> *This is the day when*
> *All of my feelings changed*
> *This is the day when*
> *All of my life till now*
> *Seemed oh so strange*

Another hint, a little broader this time in this second part of the chorus.

You know I feel like a bird of
A different feather
A trail that runs forever
Though a forest of evergreen

And using the same word structure, he talks of how his life has changed and is heading to the future. And he likes the way if feels. This is followed by some ringing acoustic and electric guitar solos that only add to and enhance the mood of the lyrics. It's one of my favorite songs by Al Stewart. You can sample a 30 second clip of the song by heading to the song page of this on Last.fm This is but a small part of what inspires me. Whether to write, be a better husband, friend, worker, whatever…we all need inspiration and music, Al's in particular, inspires me greatly.

Writer's Block: My Favorite Craft (2008-02-01 10:32)

LJ Question: What's your favorite arts & crafts project?

Not being an Artsy Craftsy kinda guy, this is a bizarre question to answer. However, I do maintain a scrapbook of Sports Stadium postcards from around the country. Football and Baseball stadiums, mostly. I've been accumulating the postcards for years, and my wife gave me the scrapbook for this past Christmas. It was a fun few days arranging and mounting the cards, along with a few ticket stubs. Makes a nice way to keep them all together and presentable.

Letter to Gramdma (2008-02-01 15:07)

Dear Grandma,

It's been a year, Grandma.
A year since you went to be with Jesus.
A year since I saw you smile,
    or that twinkle in your eye.
A year since I heard you laugh,
    or say, "Oh Honestly!" because
    somebody did something, when they
    should have known better.
A year since you had dessert,
    or worried about your weight.
It's been a year since I told you I love you,
    or heard you say the same.
It's been a long year, Grandma.

Was your reunion with Granddad joyful?
Can Mother walk? And dance? And Sing?
Have you seen your Sister or Father or Mother?
Have you told my wife's parents that she misses them?
    And that I do as well?
Has the love of your Lord Jesus wrapped you in bliss
    as you walk those streets of gold?

Do you know how much I miss you, Grandma?
Do you ever hear me cry?

It's been a year now, Grandma.
A year since we said goodbye...

    Godspeed, Grandma

Writer's Block: My Own Creation (2008-02-02 11:03)

LJ Question: If you could create anything artistic, what would it be?

As I can't paint anything beyond a cabinet, that would be fun to learn. I'd also like to leave some lasting contribution to the world of literature. Doesn't matter what form it takes. That will grow out of my writing, I hope. I also believe that being a friend is an art of some sort. The artistry of love, trust and belief in somebody is priceless, in my estimation.

Writer's Block: Love This Artist (2008-02-03 11:22)

LJ Question: Who is your favorite artist?

If we're talking painting, then it would be Gil Elvgren. He could paint women in a sexy way, in an understated idealized way, that wasn't exploitive or degrading (to my eye) fashion. They looked like the girl next door, and there's a sense of innocence in his paintings. Other artists I like quite a lot include Mike Worley (also a nice guy), Rick Stasi, Charles M. Russell (I have a glorious print of his work that hangs in our living room), Will Eisner, r stevens, my Great-Grandmother (scads of her works on our walls), and the cross-stitch work of both my Wife and my Mother-in-Law. When they complete a project, and frame it, it's beautiful to behold. In a completely different vein, Friend of he Blog, Jade does some compelling and interesting work. She says a lot in her work, using a minimum of colors. I find it evocative and quite beautiful.

Dost Thou LibraryThing? (2008-02-04 09:55)

I got one hell of a lot of books. Books on all sorts of subjects and genres. Well, maybe not as wide a selection of subjects and genres as I thought originally. I'm also a bit compulsive and when the chance to catalog something comes along, I jump at it. Completing said projects can be a different matter, but that's neither here nor there. I found this spiffy web site called LibraryThing.org and they provide a platform for cataloging books that you own or have read. Some people just list books they've read (and the totals are staggering) while there are folks like me who start, and sort of limp along. It can be a daunting task, even with a keypad and ISBN numbers to help you along.

Here is my profile on LibraryThing and at present, it's long on pulps. Those tawdry, gaudily covered rags of plot driven prose. Some of it was as purple as a people eater, and some was quite good. Dashiell Hammett gained his notoriety through the Pulps. In fact, The Maltese Falcon was originally run as a serial in Black Mask. There is also a good bit of sports books, and there will be more as that's a particular passion of mine. I have just sort of been entering piles or small shelves of my "collection" (accumulation would be more appropriate) at random moments. There is no rhyme or reason, just sort of what I feel like at that moment.

I find it a useful tool, but I don't think it will become a huge social networking success like Last.fm or Facebook has. Not as many people read books as listen to music or collect DVD's and the like. Another thing I've noticed is there seems to be a dropoff in cataloging around the mid 100's or so. I would suppose that is a breakoff point for the uncommitted, or they realize what a task it is.

Finally, I only have a couple of brick bats to toss in their direction and that's web site related. Firstly, there is no automated notification system when there is a friend request, or a comment left on your profile page. Something sent to my inbox would be nice. Secondly, you're provided the chance to sign up for a lifetime membership for the low price of $25. Not a lot in the big picture, but nowhere does the site explain the benefits of this or the drawbacks of being a free member. I found this to be a shortcoming that should be addressed.

http://www.librarything.com/profile/yingko

Letters? Letters? (2008-02-05 10:54)

Does anyone still write letters anymore? I like to write them, but since I seldom get responses, it makes it difficult to get jazzed about actually writing more. There's just something permanent and personal about writing a letter, putting it in an envelope, addressing it, and mailing it. There's a heft and weight to a letter that can never be replaced by email or online journal entries. Letters are so very, "for your eyes only" in the way that electronic messages aren't. There's a connection when you hold a letter in your hand with the writer of that letter. You know that they held that paper in their hands, that they cared enough to sit down and physically write to you. Since writing it down on paper entails commitment that isn't present in electronic communication (much more permanent), or a phone call, people tend to think more about what they pen on paper. So, the communication is more considered, more thoughtful and most likely more personal as a result.

I've been carrying on a correspondence with my 97 year Grandmother. She can't see too well, has to have somebody read them to her, but they mean the world to her. I also enjoy getting her letters, and I keep and treasure them. At some point, they will be the only physical link I have to her, as I read them again in the future. Again, it's that tactile thing that seems to resonate with me. I love the feel of letters in my hands when I read them.

Sadly, and this is a trend that started long before the internet became so prevalent, people don't write nearly as many letters as they used to. Which is sad to me. I have a brown paper grocery sack of letters my Grandfather wrote my Grandmother from the time when they were courting throughout their married life. Whenever he traveled on business, he took time to write to her. It's a nice way of walking through their life together and something that is rapidly disappearing from our lives.

I Like Beer (2008-02-06 09:59)

This is one of the better country songs of the 70's. Written and sung with tongue firmly planted in cheek by The Storyteller, Tom T. Hall, it's an ode to suds. A list of why he prefers beer to other intoxicants that is just a happy, cheerful and funny little ditty to barley pop. Give it a listen.

Writer's Block: Coffee Or Tea? (2008-02-06 11:42)

LJ Question: What method do you use to prepare your coffee or tea?

Boiling water in the cup, with leaves in the infuser. When I travel, I tote along a plastic box of tea bags. It's less messy.

Damn, that was cold... (2008-02-08 19:52)

Last weekend, my buddy Pat and I went to Jefferson City (Capital of Our Great State) which is 30 miles or so south of here to look at motorcycle helmets and a bike for him. I already have two of each, and don't need another of either (Not that I need the ones I have, but that's a discussion for another time. Maybe), but I was there to help in any way I could. He ended up choosing one of each for him, and he took along the brain bucket, leaving the bike there to think about it, check out funding and a call on Tuesday.

Tuesday finds a "Sold" hung on the bike, funding has been secured and we wait until Friday to go and get it, He works Sunday through Thursday, whilst I took the afternoon off. Before I joined him and his wife, I went to Fuddrucker's for lunch with some other friends, two of which are having birthdays this month (yay for birthdays!). Much laughing, munching and hilarity ensued. Then I left. I've no clue what happened there after that, but I went home, put on an extra pair of socks and got the rest of my cold riding gear together.

Last Monday (don't you just love skipping around in time? Think of the paradoxes!) It was around 73 degrees, so I took the afternoon off to go riding my motorcycle. I hauled out the Wing, and headed out on the highway. About 20 miles in, I blew a fuse. I changed it, and got about a mile and the same fuse blew again. Frustrating? You bet. Especially since it was the back running lights. I didn't have anymore fuses of that type in the saddlebags, so I headed for home. Bummer, dude. I was going to haul out the other bike and get some miles on it, but I was too tired and irritated. So, I punted that idea and waited until my wife got off work so I could pick her up from work.

I have a draggy brake pad on the front wheel, or at least it sounds like that, and I had all the front "tupperware" (the plastic outer shell on the front of the bike) off the bike last fall so I could change plugs and air filter and when I got finished, I couldn't get the reverse lever (Reverse? On a Motorcycle? Thing weighs 900 pounds. You back it up a small hill with your feet) back on, and it needs a state inspection. So, since I was going to be at the shop to ride Pat's new bike home, I figured I'd take mine there to get repaired (Don't you love when a story comes together?).

It was overcast, windy and 47 degrees when I left home. I met up with my friends halfway to Jefferson City and they followed me to Larry's Motor Sports. It was chilly, but not horrible. It threatened to rain, the windshield got wet a couple of times, and I considered putting on the rain suit. However, it stopped and I didn't. I took care of my business, Pat took care of his, and off we went.

The ride to his house was quite different than the ride there. Namely because a Gold Wing GL1500 is a luxury touring bike. It's essentially a

Fairing and Luggage with a cushy seat, two wheels, and a six-cylinder engine. Heck, I can listen to my iPod without much trouble. Pat's Honda Shadow, which is a great bike and quite like it, ain't a Gold Wing. It's a metric cruiser. Knees in the breeze and the whole ball of wax. So, I was getting hit with wind. Lots of if.

Still, for all that, it wasn't a bad ride. Wouldn't want to take that bike or my C50 from St. Louis to Kansas City without heated britches or a pair of chaps, but the 30 miles back to his place wasn't bad. My toes got cold, even with two pair of socks, but not uncomfortably so. Actually, the biggest problem I had was my riding gloves cutting into my wrist. I never thought I'd ride a motorcycle with temperatures in the mid 40's, under overcast skies and a chance of rain. Hardly ideal conditions. But I wasn't the only nut out there. I passed 4 other riders today. I'd do it all over again, and I'll be they would too.

Walls to Nowhere (2008-02-09 16:20)

I ignored you,
Or so it seemed to you.
An invisible wall,
That you couldn't see;
That I wouldn't fight.

You ignore me,
Or is it something else?
A one way mirror,
That you're peering through;
That reflects back to me.

I reach to you,
Over the mists of time.
Hoping to connect,
To start us talking;
To heal that rift.

Writer's Block: A Favorite Poem (2008-02-11 09:13)

LJ Question: What is one of your favorite poems?

How bizarre that this be the question today. I just bought a couple of poetry books over the weekend. As to my favorite poem, the only one I've ever memorized was written by a camp counselor, whose name I can no longer recall. We were on a camping trip in the wilds of Ontario when he regaled us with this comical little ditty. I had him write it out for me, as I really liked it.

>Sometimes falling forward on my butt,
>I blunder
>
>Sometimes calling silently to space,
>I wonder,
>
>Oh what the hell!
>It doesn't matter anymore!
>Oh what the hell!
>I've said it all before!
>
>But!
>
>Sometimes falling forward on my butt,
>I wonder,
>Isn't this ass on backwards?

I'm pretty certain that's how it went...

Other poems I like include "The Daffodils" by Wordsworth. It hangs on the wall in our home, nicely crosstitched. So much of poetry confuses me because I'm so literal in my thinking at times. I have a hell of a time divining the meaning from what some poets say or are trying to say. Which probably explains my liking of Cowboy Poetry. It's direct and simple. No guessing or serious thinking involved which makes it more amusing for me. I have a couple of volumes of Cowboy poetry and one of my favorite poets in that field is Omar S. Barker. He not only wrote passable western pulp fiction, but was a good cowboy poet. Well, there ya go. My feeble thoughts on poetry. Time for some tea.

Damn... (2008-02-11 20:32)

I read a few minutes ago that Steve Gerber died yesterday. Who? Who the hell is Steve Gerber, you ask?

Somebody who warped my mind as a kid, and somebody I admired for that and am grateful for doing that for me. Y'see, Steve Gerber created one of my favorite funny books when I was a kid. Howard the Duck was the character and the comic. "Trapped in a world he never made" was the series tag line, and was something I could identify with as a teenager.

Remember, this took place in the 70's and the Rose Colored Glasses of 50's Nostalgia was running amok in popular culture. "Grease", "Happy Days", "Laverne & Shirley", "American Graffiti" and other items of looking back-ness. Things were better then, and it did indeed look as if the future was a tad murky and scary.

Further, being a teenager was hard enough. Being different was the kiss of death, from a social standpoint. And Gerber's whacked out Howard made it "okay" to be different. Well, maybe not okay but it gave me some hope. I mean, he had a babe for a girlfriend, was a master of Quack Fu and fought Dr. Bong! How cool was that? How funny was that? (Dr. Bong! What a hysterical name....)

I didn't know satire from a flat tire, but I knew funny and strange. And Howard the Duck was funny and strange and that was a direct result of Steve Gerber's writing, wit and eye for skewering pop culture. He was easily as good a satirist as Charles Dickens, even if he did ply his bric bat throwing in a different medium.

I was delighted to find that Gerber was writing a current series I've been reading from the beginning, "Countdown to Mystery" and it features Dr. Fate. Sadly, he won't be finishing that mini series. Godspeed, Steve Gerber and thanks for the memories.

Writer's Block: Hard to Say I'm Sorry (2008-02-13 10:10)

LJ Question: Is there anything you've done that you wish you'd apologized for, but didn't?

I wish to hell I'd apologized to my daughter years ago. Without being told I should would also have been a good thing. For somebody who is allegedly smart as hell, I've been real stupid in some parts of life. No big surprise there. Most people do dumb things from time to time. I just do dumb things and then compound them by being stupid and thoughtless on top of it. Served up with a side of cluelessness. Seems like a Blue Plate Special of thoughtless behavior at times. Get 'em while they're hot!

Feh!

I've worked hard not to be the self-centered cad I used to be. Still, past sins haunt me and probably always will. They keep me humble.

Writer's Block: Love Is... (2008-02-14 13:21)

LJ Question: Who or what do you really love?

I love my wife. Without question, reservation or strings.
I love my daughter. Without question, reservation or strings.
I love them both simply because they are.
    Well, that and my wife smells good.

I love the rest of my family; In-laws, Out-laws and the other kind. Ones I was born with.
Those still here and departed.
I love them simply because they are as well
    I love little fuzzy ducks...(oh wait, that's already been done....)

I love my friends. They know who they are, and if they don't, that doesn't diminish my love for them.

I love baseball, but not like I love the above people. I love it in a totally different way.
I love to read, and listen to music and listen to the rain, and the sounds of snowfall as it gently rustles on its trip to the ground.
I love a good steak, medium rare. I love hot tea and iced tea. I love to ride motorcycles and to hang out with my friends.
I love being with my wife. She makes me smile, laugh and better. She completes me.

Book Review: Johnny U by Tom Callahan (2008-02-14 22:40)

I enjoy reading biographies, and I also enjoy reading about sports. So, this seemed like perfect book for me. And it was, but for reasons unrelated to football. The reason this is so, is John Unitas.

Author Callahan states that this book is as much about a team, and a time as much as it is a biography about Unitas. He's right. And that team was more than just a collection of individuals, but a team in a sense we don't see much anymore. There were few grandstanders and plenty of players willing to do what was good for the team. It's also the tale of a man, who was at the center of it

The story tells of a boy, who grew up poor, but didn't let that daunt him. Hard work, belief in himself, a bit of luck and he succeeded in being one of the greatest quarterbacks in the history of the NFL. He became an icon of not only a team, but an era. The 1950's and 1960's. An era that brought much change and moved the NFL to the dominant sports league we know today. Unitas was a part of, and left behind that change. That was as much a part of the man he was as anything else.

There is a good bit of football action talked about, but an equal amount of space and time is left to focus on his teammates, how they felt about him and who they were as well. It really is a book as much about a team, its time as well as a book about Johnny U.

While no saint, Unitas was a stand up guy. Loved and respected by many who knew him, which is a testament to his skills as not only a quarterback and a leader on the field, but to the man he was the rest of the time. He was a compelling man, and this makes for a compelling story. Which is wonderfully told by Callahan as he covers a lot of ground in a page turning fashion. Hardly a definitive biography, but certainly an entertaining one and one worthy of your time. Whether you are a football fan or not.

Coffee Break (2008-02-15 15:47)

Old Men drinking coffee
Telling lies they've told before

Well worn patterns in the stories
Take them to a time before

When they were younger
And much stronger
Than they are today

Wistfully remembering days
of other things
When drinking coffee and
Telling lies was in a
Far off time

Writer's Block: Happily Ever After? (2008-02-15 19:26)

I skipped out of work a bit early, paid a bill that needed paying, then wandered over to one of the jewelers in town. After chatting with the young lady who was helping me, I picked out a pair of earrings and matching pendant for my valentine. I cleaned out the car, washed it, stopped to pick her up some roses (yellow ones. They were so pretty), and went to her place of employment to rescue her from another day at the office. I gave her the carefully and attractively wrapped baubles which she unwrapped quickly and efficiently. The moment when the box was opened was worth it.

We went out for a wonderful dinner at the HuHot (Yay! Mongolian BBQ!) and then....

Then.....

Then we did what many married couples do at the end of a mildly romantic evening....with a warm feeling in the belly and in our hearts.....

We went to Wal-Mart!

A nice evening all the way around....

Writer's Block: It's Hard to Describe (2008-02-17 12:14)

LJ Question: What is one thing you struggle to describe?

I can't describe faces worth two cents. At least beyond the basic wide mouth, big nose, squinty, beady little eyes kind of things.

A Bike on the Flagpole (2008-02-17 12:25)

Home life growing up wasn't an ideal situation. Although I realize that most people don't grow up in an ideal setting, there are those who were more comfortable in their home and for certain those who had it worse than we did. We never wanted for food, clothing of good quality, shelter or medical care. Our parents loved us, but they both had issues and things were a mess at times. Our mother had emotional problems, and spent a few years in the house, without leaving much and while our father was there in body, he'd checked out emotionally a long time before. It was also rough because of the personalities of the two parents and the two kids. Mother was for certain a dominant personality, and Dad wasn't. She argued and he didn't come from that sort of background. They were quite different in temperment and background, and this made things hard for both of them. Add in the fact that I became a troubled child right about the time my sister was born (or, you can call it what it really was at the time, simple jealousy) and you have a home that is far from happy.

My sister Kate and I were alternately friends and enemies. In hindsight, I was far from the protective brother. In fact, I was needlessly and at times recklessly cruel to her. She didn't deserve it as she didn't go out of her way to be a nuisance, she was at times just a handy target for my frustrations. I wish to hell I didn't have to admit it, but anything else would be disingenuous at best, and at worst, an outright lie.

It was my last day of the 6th Grade at Bader Elementary, and the sun was out. It was a pretty day, the perfect day to end my time in elementary school and look forward to the adventure of Jr. High School. It was also the perfect day to pick on my sister. So, I did.

At some point, somebody had run a bike up the flagpole at the end of a school day. It was pretty funny to see a bicycle atop the flag pole, so I figured I'd have to do that to my sister's Free Spirit bike sometime. Knowing her lock combination made it extremely easy to get her bike over to the flagpole. A couple of classmates to help hoist it up while I attached the bike to the rope. It actually was fairly easy to take the clips that attached to the rings in the flag, feeding it through the spokes and wrapping it around the tire and rim a few times. Then, fastening the clip to the rope, and haul away. A girls Free Spirit bike was pretty heavy. But, I hauled it up, tied the rope off and left. Bike dangling in the breeze.

I also left my sister there. She'd stood there the entire time, almost begging me not to do this thing. I paid her no attention and continued on with my little torture. I then left her at school, laughing at my cleverness and went home. Kate walked home. It wasn't far, but it had to be a long walk fueled by anger at me. Helluva way for her summer vacation to start.

As I recall, out Mother wasn't overly happy with me, but wasn't yelling angry either. I was told to go back to school, get her bike down and bring it home. I believe I rode it home (riding a girl's bike! Ack!) and chuckled over it for a few days.

As the years go by, I remember the bike up the flagpole as a prank. In reality, it was something more. It was just another in a line of dirty tricks that I inflicted on Kate. She was in the 4th grade, and I'm not only taking away her bike ride home, but embarrassing her as well.

I'm certain that none of this was conscious thought at the time on her part, but put it together and there's a lot of reason to be angry with me. All of this has been running around in my head as I've tried to think this story through. So much more than just a simple story of running a bike up a flagpole.

Broken Circle (2008-02-20 14:43)

I love you though
I know you not.
You are of me and
    of God
And, of course, yourself.

You hate me though
You know me not.
I am of you and
    of God
and, of course, us all.

This broken circle,
That never ends,
    or starts;
Can only be fixed
    by You

I did not do it.
I did not break
It, but I did not
Try to fix it
    at all.
Until now.

You hate me though
I do not blame you.
I am so lonely
    for You.
That at night, I weep.

I love you though
I know you not.
That you are
    is enough
    for Me.

Pass the Geritol, Please (2008-02-22 11:08)

It's official. I am now...Old.

I know what the calender says, but since *cough, cough* is the new *sputter* I didn't pay it any mind. The gray in the hair, and the odd aches and pains, coupled with having to take medication for problems most 20 somethings have never heard of didn't really register. Or make an impression. I mean, I have motorcycles, I buy new music and I try to stay current. Heck, I wear earrings!

This morning, my carefully fabricated tissue of self-deception came tumbling down. Hard and fast. I met my age-related Waterloo.

My lovely and long suffering wife (she's married to me, remember?) and I stop at the local Sonic Drive-in most mornings to get a jumbo diet coke with cherry flavoring (that would be pop to you who live amongst the unclean). Nectar of the Gods, I tell ya. We've been doing this for some years and we know most of the staff, and the new ones learn who we are faster than we learn who they are, it seems. This morning, the new Car Hop brought our vessels of liquid joy to us, and told us, " I think it's cute that you two ride to work together." CUTE! AUGH! My wife and I have been reduced to CUTE in the eyes of young people! The shame! The humiliation! Oh, the horror of it all! Babies are cute! Puppies are cute! Boy band singers are cute! Hell, I was cute once. When I was...yep...you guessed it...younger.

Damn. I guess this is the Karma I get for saying the same thing to "older couples" when I was younger...

Writer's Block: I'd Like to Thank... (2008-02-24 12:16)

LJ Question: Write your Academy Awards acceptance speech.

Um....right.....thanks. Are you fucking serious?

<Exit Stage Left>

Shoelaces (2008-02-24 13:40)

My fingers are strawberries
Soaking in battery acid
As my mind wanders
Down frosted corridors
Of wet electricity. (so bright)
Nothing and everything
Makes sense all at once,
As my toes blossom
Into yellow daffodils.
Pollen trailing in the
River of Possibilities that flows around
My knees of concrete. (so hard)
Overhead in the sky
Of pudding dripping
Slowly down, drowning
The roses and dandelions
That grow out of my scalp.
I am aware.
I am at peace.
I am well blended.
I should like to go to
The dark side of the moon,
To meet Mr. Pink
As the lava flows in the vacuum of eternity.
I hear the silence (so loud)
And it makes me shriek.
Milk flows down my cheeks
As I laugh at the void In the paper or plastic
That is my shoe.

We All Fall Down (2008-02-24 13:51)

Camelot has crumbled.
The Shining City on a Hill Is run down. the
Thousand Points of Light Blinding us to the tarnish.
Government that is of the People is now
Government Buy the People
Not For the People, and in
Spite of The People.

Fear itself would be better
Than the Fear of our Leaders
That we have allowed with our Blindness.
We are in danger of perishing
From This Earth, due to
The lethargy we allow
And encourage.

We beat our breasts
And pound our drums
March off to war in
The Name of Freedom.
Lying to them, and
Worst of all, Ourselves.

Government that is now
Of The People,
Bought through Some People
is not for The People,
but To the People.
There is no freedom in that.

Camelot is in ruins.
Those dreams faded to dust.
The Shining City on the Hill
Is a vague memory
As the Thousand Points of Light
One by one, go out

With no apologies to Lincoln, FDR, Kennedy, Reagen or Bush the First.

Writer's Block: Sticks and Stones (2008-02-25 20:11)

LJ Question: What's the meanest thing you've ever said to someone?

I told some ass hat that he was a good argument for retro-active abortion. Some other yahoo really pissed me off, so I told him the best part of him ran down his mothers legs... Then I grew up and don't break bad on people like that anymore.

Writer's Block: Since I had to pick something... (2008-02-26 08:42)

LJ Question: What aspect of your personality could use a little work?

I dunno if this is a personality thing or not, but I do need to get better at dealing with direct confrontation. This means, when there's a problem, instead of just hoping it will go away, I need to do something about it. It's this serious flaw in my character that has lead to a serious problem I see no way of resolving anytime soon. Other than that, I'm a hell of a guy. Just ask me, I'll be happy to tell you! ;-) (Did I just say that?)

From the Vaults (2008-02-26 09:09)

We went to San Francisco in 2004, and it was a marvelous experience. I can see why so many people love the city and the area. It's beautiful, or at least the parts we saw. I suggest riding over the [1]Golden Gate in a firetruck, if you can. It's a great ride...

On one of our last nights, we went to Baker Beach and I just stood there. Looking at the opening of the bay, and the ocean, with the cliffs across the channel, and the bridge disappearing in the fog. It was an amazing moment. I hauled out my little Moleskinne and wrote this down;

<u>Baker Beach</u>

It sings to me
        A one note tune
Volume and tempo
        Are all that change

The wind joins in
        The chord of a foghorn too
But the one note song
        Is the song That I hear call.

Dunno what to think about it. Thoughts?

1. http://www.fireenginetours.com/

Now begins the wait... (2008-02-27 12:29)

I did it. I submitted a couple of poems for consideration to be published this morning. Neither has been posted here for the general public to read. It seems kind of strange submitting something electronically, but it works for me.

It's been 20 years or so since I had stones enough to submit something. Last time, I got a rejection note. Which is appropriate. That story was awful, to be honest. Although, it did prefigure the current Vampire craze by about 10 years.

Well, anyhow...wish me luck.

(as an aside, I never got a response from them. Apparently, they closed)

Kind of a rough night (2008-02-27 22:03)

It's a rough night around here. My wife's eldest sister called tonight. She had some really sad news to share. Their oldest brother died a few days ago. Alone. He was discovered today by a maintenance worker who works at the apartment complex where he was living. Where he died. Alone. It's the 'Alone' part that bothers me more than anything. Nobody should die alone. I know it happens, but it's one of those things in life that saddens me. One of those things I can't do anything about. Alone.

I'm not really sure what to feel right now. I didn't know him very well and hadn't seen him in over a year. He lived across town from us. My wife hadn't seen him since sometime last year, and they weren't particularly close. Still, it's quite sad. Now there is no time to get to know him better. Or to see him again. Hear him laugh. Or talk.

I guess I'm really bummed that my brother-in-law passed away and that I don't feel like the world has ended. That it doesn't hurt more than it does. I'm sad for his sons (both grown) and the grand babies. I know the loss of a parent. You're never old enough for it. I hurt for my wife who is hurting more than she is letting on. I'm sad for the rest of the in-laws who have lost a family member. I grieve for them.

R.I.P. Tommy...

The Sun'll Come Out, Tomorrow! (2008-02-29 16:30)

Hooray! Finally! Yee-stinkin'-hah!!

I get to get the Gold Wing out of the shop tomorrow and ride it! Ever since I put it there, the weather has been awful. Dreadful, to be honest. And there's a call for snow showers on Monday! After 70 degree weather on Sunday. This has been the most unreal, surreal, bizarre winter I can recall here in Central Missouri.

I admit it. I'm hooked. (2008-02-29 20:40)

Most people get hooked on TV shows. I've been hooked, at various times, to shows as diverse as Buffy The Vampire Slayer to the really obscure shows like Skag. However, the current obsession is How It's Made. Which is really embarrassing.

It is really a simple premise. The producers come up with all sorts of simple, everyday items and show you how they're made. From items like Traditional Snow Shoes to Outboard Motors, to things like pocket knives or flatware. This show covers it all. I've seen how brass bells are made. It was really fascinating, but who came up with the idea of showing people how it's made? Who thinks of things like that?

One thing I've found is that there are some manufacturing techniques that work with various applications. Which is really pretty neat, when you stop and think about it for more than 12 seconds. The ingenuity involved in creating manufacturing process's for such a wide array of products shows to me how intelligent the Man/Woman can be.

Oh, and did you know that there is Mineral Oil inside those gray transformers that are on light poles? Me either.

Book Review: The Case of the Curious Bride
by Earl Stanley Gardner
(2008-03-01 06:56)

It's a shame that there is a generation or two of people who have never heard of Mr. Gardner. They've heard of his creation, and quite possibly have never seen a TV show, TV movie or earlier film featuring him, yet his entrance into the popular culture was so complete and deeply rooted that even today, everybody knows that Perry Mason is a terrific lawyer.

Gardner started his series in the 1930's, and if read today, there is a lot of material that is dated in the original novels. (An example would be seeing the cars registration on the steering column) I remember watching Perry Mason shows with Raymond Burr when I was a kid. The story always followed along similar lines, crime, detection, the trial, and a confession on the stand and Mason defeats the idiot D.A. yet again. Mason was all about justice, and on the side of the angels.

Not so in the books. Mason is of a dubious moral quality, but he'll fight like a tiger for what HE believes is right. And he's up to his usual hijinks in this novel, originally published in 1934. Here's the blurb from the back cover:

> *After con man Greg Moxley married Rhoda Lorton, he took her money and flew-only to have his plane crash. Years later, Rhoda wed millionaire scion Carl Montaine. But now Moxley has turned up alive and well...with plans to pocket the Montaine fortune-or else make Rhoda's bigamy public. Desperate to protect the good name of Montaine, Rhoda seeks out Perry Mason. But before Mason can reel in Moxley, somebody murders the scheming blackmailer. In a case that abounds in lethal twists, Mason suddenly finds himself on a collision course with a cold-blooded killer.*

Mason plays fast and loose with legal loopholes, evidence and witnesses. Like all the Mason novels I've read, the action is non-stop, the pacing frantic and the characters built on quickly recognizable archetypes. Gardner wrote solid pot boiler novels. This is one of the better books in the series. We do find out who the killer really is, and Mason does use the legal system to find this out, but not in the sanitized way the TV show would have done. While you may not agree with the way he does things, you will enjoy reading the story to find out the who, what, why and where.

Ain't Never the Same Ride Twice (2008-03-01 22:19)

Those words occurred to me this afternoon on an off ramp. My buddy Greg and I were exiting I-70, and it was windy as all get out. I have a tank bag with some strong magnets. Didn't matter, as the wind almost ripped that bag off the gas tank twice. That would've have been bye-bye to my cheap cell phone, my all important Moleskinne and a Mickey Spillane paperback. I've no idea why I had a paperback with me on a motorcycle ride, but I did. And it was in the tank bag that was trying to fly off my bike on I-70. That's never happened before.

Which is why I realized that even if you go down the same road multiple times on a bike, it's never the same ride twice. Unlike riding in a car, there are more things to keep track of when riding a motorcycle. What's on the road, for example. Roadkill is more than just something that stinks, it can kill you if you're not careful. There is also the problem of gravel on the road, which can help you really meet the road. That causes serious rashes. Road rash...(shudder)

The other thing that can affect a ride is the weather. It's more than temperature, it's all the other aspects of the weather. Rain is no fun, even with a rain suit. That makes it barely tolerable, not fun. High heat and humidity makes wearing protective clothing uncomfortable, but I'd not ride without it. It takes a special sort to ride in the snow and sub freezing temperatures. I am not that special.

Today was beautiful. Partly cloudy and mid 60's. Not the middle of January mid 60's where you have strong indications of winter, like the odd breath of cold air, but hints and whispers of spring that are in the air as winters grip loosens. Today was also quite windy. Hence the attempts at flying by the tank bag. After riding 10 miles on I-70 with one hand on the throttle and one hand on the bag (couldn't lose my paperback), we stopped and I shoved the whole thing into a saddlebag and away we went.

Greg and I rose close to 100 miles together. We wandered down quiet 2 lane country roads, soaking up the day as we rode through it. We passed a couple of aromatic hog farms, and a dead skunk but also saw some geese and grazing cattle. There was also quite a few other motorcycles out and about today. The cabin fever and P.M.S. (parked motorcycle syndrome) was being cured, if only for a while today.

Up and down, and round short and long sweeping curves we rode. Listening to the music of the wind whipping past our helmets and the rumble of the exhaust of both bikes. A spring symphony of mechanical freedom.

I spent most of the afternoon either riding the Gold Wing home from the shop, or out on the C50 with Greg. It was almost like Summer. Of course, first we have Spring to look forward to.

My wonderful wife spent the afternoon doing something she enjoyed. She went shopping. I got a couple of new ball caps out of it. And she was smiling when I got home. Which is better than anything else. All around, it was a good day.

Writer's Block: Go Get 'Em? (2008-03-02 08:07)

LJ Question: Are you a go-getter or do you wait for things to happen to you?

Yeah, pretty much.

To Buy Some Lettuce (2008-03-02 22:22)

Quite a day today. Rode to the local breakfast eatery for some breakfast (novel idea, that). Once finished, I rode home, after a stop at the Subway sandwich shop to purchase a sandwich (yet another stellar notion!), and I rode on home, full of breakfast and sandwich in tank bag (which was not wishing to fly) for my wife (what? You think I'm some sort of pig?).

After she ate her sandwich, and I answered some email, we left the house and headed to Rocheport. A small river town about 15 miles down I-70 to the west. I passed the exit twice (going out and coming back) yesterday. Sorry, I digress.

Well, this time, I took the exit and down into Rocheport we went. We didn't go on two wheels, but rather we went on four. And all four were stopped when I out the van in park in the parking lot near the KATY Trail, which is the reason we went to Rocheport in the first place.

Well then, there we were in Rocheport, having driven there so we would be there, and there we were! I like it when a plan works out so well. Don't you? So, we get out of the van and commence to walk down the KATY Trail, heading in a westerly direction. I would not have enjoyed riding a bicycle on the trail today as the ground was firm enough for walking, but the tire tracks of other people who did ride bicycles (proving, as if there was any real need, that I am far smarter than they) were much deeper than you would expect on a walking and biking trail. However, we've a lot of rain/snow/freezing rain/sleet and general cats and dogs falling out of the sky and littering the landscape and so the ground everywhere is pretty soggy. More rain and snow in the forecast for tonight through Tuesday. That's going to be a huge help in drying out the KATY Trail, isn't it? Again, I digress.

There is a tunnel, the only on from the days of the MKT Railroad when they owned and operated the rail line. The construction is pretty interesting, if you stop to take a look. The east entrance looks just like a domed cut out. Sort of all rough and like that, with soot stains from the passage of old steam locomotives. The west entrance, on the other hand, has a stone face, and the arch is filled with the same type of large stone, and for part of the way, the ceiling is covered with bricks. Why it was built like this, I have no idea. The other interesting fact about this tunnel, is the movie "Sometimes They Come Back" which is based on a Stephen King story, was filmed in Boonville (a nearby town with a pretentious attitude). The scene where the car comes after them? That's the tunnel. It's niftier to look at in person.

It was a lovely day out. Temps in the upper 70's and strong winds. It was great to be outside, walking along this sort of sloppy trail, yet not getting all gross and stuff. It was great to out in nature, but with winter unwilling to loosen its grip, everything was essentially the color of winter, which is gray. Naked trees are gray, the rotting leaves have turned gray, the sky was sort of gray (except where it wasn't, then it was kind of blue. Come to think of it, that's sort of close to gray...). It just seemed without much change in the color scheme that everything was sort of two dimensional. Now, I don't want to give the idea that it wasn't wonderful outside, it was. It's just that it was all a big tease. A promise of what is yet to come, but not yet. Not quite yet, kiddies. Enjoy it while you can. I could have confused the winds howling through the trees and the tunnel with some sinister laughter if I went in for that sort of thing. Which I don't. But, if I did...well, you get the idea.

So, where was I? Oh yeah, we amble around for a while, then we amble back to the parked van. After unlocking the van and getting in, we head for home. That, of course, assumes that you know without my telling you that I actually started the thing up. Right? Right. Good...

After being at home for a while, we discussed that since I had devoured the last of the salad, if we were going to have more with our dinner, we needed to get some lettuce. They sell that at the grocery store, and I was wanting to get my wife to go on a motorcycle ride with me. So, I told her we were going to go to the grocery store to get some lettuce and peppers and dressing and such. And go on the Gold Wing. She asked if that was all? If we were going any further than that and I said no. Just the grocery store. In Centralia (We live in Columbia. That's 15 miles away from where we live).

Now, I have to digress (yet again. I checked my calendar, and somewhere, it's National Digression Day. You mean it's not? Damn! Oh well, this is my LJ, and if I want to digress like a book junkie at Half Price Books, that's okay fine) because you probably don't know that my wife isn't nearly as fond of motorcycles as I am. In fact, you could probably go so far as to say she's not real fond of them. Period. However, she does go for short rides around town with me on the Gold Wing (which I particularly enjoy) from time to time. She hadn't been out with me yet this year because it wasn't warm enough for her. Fair enough. 78 degrees today was warm enough. Going to Centralia wasn't. But, after some discussion (and pouting and whining on my part), she caved in just to shut me up and away we went. 16 miles there to Prenger's and 16 miles back from Prenger's. We got our lettuce, I got my wife to ride with me on a pretty day, we went for a long leisurely walk on the KATY Trail, and we have a funeral to go to tomorrow and a snow storm is coming.

Writer's Block: Grounded. (2008-03-03 19:08)

LJ Question: What was the last thing you were grounded for?

I haven't been grounded in nearly 30 years. What the hell kind of fool question is this?

My Sister (2008-03-04 12:32)

I know I've written about my sister before. She's a terrific lady and I'm very proud of her. She has done well with her life. She has a husband who is a good man, not only to her but their children as well. Heck, he's even nice to me! I'd say the same about my wife, but everyone likes her, to that's not unusual.

Sis is a terrific mother to her two little boys. They are pretty normal little boys, and full of boundless little boy energy, yet they are well behaved boundless energy little boys. A real pleasure to be around and lots of fun. She keeps a blog that is mostly focused on cooking. I enjoy it and she really enjoys doing it. It shows in her posts. And she has started adding pictures of her creations.

So, head on over to "[1]One Little Corner of the World" and surprise her. Tell her that her brother sent her. ;-)

1. http://cookkatie.blogspot.com/

The End Has Come (2008-03-04 21:53)

NFL Network is showing Super Bowl XXXI tonight. Makes sense since it was announced today that Brett Favre is retiring after a career that will no doubt become the stuff of Legend.

Of course, the legend has been a long time in the making. He's done things that no Quarterback in the NFL has ever done before. He did it for almost 17 years in a Packers uniform. Along with the late Reggie White, they were responsible for the resurgence of the Packers in the 90's. It was a great time to be a Packer fan.

I remember when he was a youngster with the Packers, and took over for The Magic Man, Don Majkowski in that September 1992 game. He then became the regular starter and did he light things up. It didn't matter which team you played for, he threw that ball all over the place. Anyone was likely to catch his passes. He reminded me of a young Terry Bradshaw. As likely to win you the game as lose it. Both matured as players, both retained the reckless "gunslinger" mentality and both were always fun to watch. My dad said he'd never make it, that he wasn't good enough or smart enough to learn the game. That he was too cocky and depended too much on his talent and not his smarts. I guess this is where I get to say, "Hey Dad! You sure got that one wrong, didn't you?" One of the few things he's been wrong about in my life. LOL!

I got to see him play in person 4 times. Twice at the Frozen Tundra, and twice at the god awful domed disaster in St. Louis (nice building, but football is meant to be played outdoors...). He was always fun to watch. It was a real pleasure to be in St. Louis the day he broke Dan Marino's yardage record. A special moment, to be sure.

But, I think it was time for him to move on. He got to go out on his own terms. He will be a sure fire first ballot Hall of Famer in 2013. Canton is sure to be a madhouse on that day. Favre is more than just a football player. He has transcended the game and is as much an icon and folk hero as he is a professional athlete.

Thank you for everything, Brett.

Snowstorm cancelled due to Sunshine (2008-03-05 21:20)

Ok, so over this past weekend, there was a Winter Storm Advisory with the expectation of a snow storm bringing anywhere from 2-6 inches to starting with rain, the turning into freezing rain and sleet. This was to begin Sunday night and go into Tuesday.

I'm still waiting.

All we've had since then is sunshine and warmer than expected temperatures.

How is it that Meteorologists and Economists can be wrong so damn often and still get paid? Would somebody please answer that?

What If? (2008-03-06 12:57)

This was prompted by the all unwritten community. I scrawled the first few lines, and decided to stop...and make it a Friends only thing. It has some potential, but is so maudlin...but I do maudlin well.

>What if the world was my oyster?
>With a pearl of great worth
>Resting inside, glowing madly?
>What if, Dear Child, things
>Had worked out differently?
>If I had been there?
>Would you still be Daddy's Girl?
>What if, I had been stronger?
>If I had been able to to
>Face down my demons, For You?
>The world may be my oyster,
>But that Pearl of great value
>Means little without You here...

======

How's that for mid-life teen angst?

Writer's Block: What? No Goodnight Kiss? (2008-03-06 15:52)

LJ Question: What is the worst date you've ever been on?

Long before I met my wife, I was set up on a blind date by some well meaning friends. Seemed like a good idea at the time. So, the night comes around and we go out for drinks and dinner. We have a nice time, she's smart, witty, is a good conversationalist and we have some things in common. She wasn't hard to look at, no great beauty, but the inner beauty is really what's most important. So, we end up at her place, and we're drinking a glass of wine (well, she is...I'm trying to find a plant. Wine is nasty...) and she's giving me the grand tour of the place. Nice digs and all. I'm kind of wondering what's going to happen next by this time because this is kind of different for me.

So, we end up in the living room, relaxing and talking and out of the blue she tells me that as much fun as she had, and as obviously as nice a guy as I am and all that sort of stuff (oh great, here it comes...), she would rather not see me again. The only reason being is that I don't make enough money for her to consider me anything more than somebody fun. And she's afraid she'll get attached and that it's just better if things don't go any further.

I left feeling like I got jobbed but flunked the interview...a really bizarre and at the time, bothersome experience.

Things turned out well for me in the long run, though.

Tunnel (2008-03-08 16:48)

On the KATY Trail, there is a tunnel. The Trail used to be the MKT (Missouri-Kansas-Texas) Rail line through Missouri. And the tunnel in Rocheport was the only one in the KATY system. It was used during filming of "Sometimes They Come Back" but looks less scary in the day time.

Smokin' (2008-03-11 09:42)

This past weekend I went on a dizzying used CD buying frenzy. First stop was the Public Library book and other assorted crap sale. CD's were $1 a pop. I spent $5 (how many CD's did I buy? Didn't you hate word math problems in school?) then the next stop was the local record store. They have an ongoing buy 3 get the 4th free scheme that I continually ~~get suckered into~~ take advantage of. Lots of stuff that I'd not expect to see at this record store, so I grabbed while the grabbing was good.

But, Jeebus, Jobus, and Marsie Doats...who smokes so much in their house that their CD cases reek of it? I opened one of them up (the local store kindly shrink wraps them all over again. After ~~defecating~~ decorating them up with USED stickers that are sometimes difficult to remove) and my olfactory senses were assaulted with legions of Friday Night odors. That really packed a wallop, lemme tell ya.

Musical Memories -D.R.E.A.D. (2008-03-11 19:25)

The damnedest things trigger memories or flashes. A recent conversation with somebody triggered almost total recall of D.R.E.A.D. and the card I carried proclaiming my membership thereof. What in hell is D.R.E.A.D. you ask? Good question. And why would I need a card for it? I'm gonna tell ya all about it.

The above is the immortal D.R.E.A.D. card. At least the front of one. D.R.E.A.D. stood for Detroit Rockers Engaged in the Abolition of Disco. It was a gimmick created by Detroit radio station WRIF (Rock is Fundamental) 101 FM (BABY!) I have no bloody idea what my number was, but I did have that silly thing for more than 10 years. I think it finally broke into little pieces because I didn't have sense enough to actually take it out of my wallet. I carried it to death, it seems. As you can see, it was an Anti-Disco group. Not everyone liked Disco back then. Some people really disliked it a lot. I'm sure it was more than just a musical thing. I have no doubt that there were racial overtones and anti-gay as well. But, I was just a punk kid who thought he knew more than he really did and having a D.R.E.A.D. card was cool. At least among my peers, it was. It was also a discount card at lots of places in Southeastern Michigan at the time. Harmony Records, as I recall, was one of them. I think it also was good at some more local shops, but I don't really remember.

As you can see, there was a goofy list of rules. They played on all the stereotypes of the Disco craze. Heck, I don't even remember what "The Chair" was, but it sure sounded ominous. So, I just didn't tell anyone when I wore my super cool silky shirt to the roller rink on Friday's. And nobody knew about the K.C. & The Sunshine Band record I had. And I wasn't telling, either. ;-) I don't know if anything like this would gain the same traction today as it did then. Musical tastes are much more fractured today. Station programming on the radio appears to be more narrowly directed. There is more choices available today, so there is less commonality in what people do or how they dress or listen to or watch on TV. Not a complaint from a grumpy old man, just calling it like I see it. Just a neat artifact of days gone by in one region of the country.

You find the damnedest things sometimes...
(2008-03-11 20:29)

One of the things I inherited when my grandmother passed last year was a desk. The desk was bought when my mother still lived at home and she was born in 1941, so it's a pretty old desk. It's a great desk, and I'm glad to have it. It was referred then and now as Granddad's desk. That's the way I think of it in my own mind and I'd be willing to bet that my sister does as well. Funny the way that stuff works, isn't it?

Anyhow, I was looking for a pencil to draw some silly pictures. I succeeded on both counts. Because in the desk, I found a regular pencil. I knew it had to be old, but I had no idea how old. And I'd still have no idea if I hadn't stopped to read what was printed on the pencil.

It had the basketball schedule for the Gustavus High School team. For the 1948-49 season. I can only make out the words for the games after Christmas 1948, so it's kind of incomplete. However, a pencil that old? I'm amazed it's legible at all.

I have no idea where in the country this school is located, but it's kind of cool.

EDIT: UPDATE! UPDATE! Thanks to my friend Bruce R., I know where this High School was located. In Trumball Co. in NE Ohio. Which makes sense to me...as that's the area where my Grandfather grew up. And where his mother lived for years. So, him latching onto a pencil and taking it with him, or tucking it away after his mother passed...

The High School is just a memory, as are many of the opponents. They've all been folded into a larger rural district. A fairly common happenstance

Thanks, Bruce!

Doodles the Cat (2008-03-12 10:43)

Pencil, Paper, Scanned, Posted, Ducking.

Told you I can't draw worth 2 cents.

Writer's Block: The Things We Carry (2008-03-12 14:26)

LJ Question: What do you always carry with you?

Memories. Of those that have come and gone, those that are still here and those I need to forgive. I carry remorse for those I've hurt and not been able to apologize to for it. Or attempt to make amends. Sometimes it's not enough, but to not try at all is even worse, IMHO.

Joy. The simple joy of being alive. Seeing life and the love of creation around me. Trees, whether sleeping or blooming or turning russet in the fall. Grass before it's mowed and just after. Daffodils in the spring. They make my wife smile and signal that winter is moving on. Finally. Puddles, rivers, lakes, a glass of cold beer. The laugh of a child or the laugh of somebody much older. I carry the joy of these and so much more with me always.

I carry the rarest gift of all. The love of a good woman. The complete and marvelous love of trust and friendship and more. Much more. The freedom to be myself and return home to her and be more as a man because of it. I carry the completed feeling of someone who has found the right person to journey through life with. We can disagree and not be disagreeable. Together we are more than the sum of the two of us. She completes me and keeps me grounded. It is a trust I treasure and a gift beyond compare.

I carry the Peace that passes all understanding through the love of The Savior. I don't deserve it, have done nothing to earn it and never could. I accept it for the free gift that it is. I cry at how many use It as a cudgel to force others to behave the way they see fit. This grieves me as I don't see this as the love of Our Savior, but something else.

I carry these things in my heart everywhere I go. The rest of the crap I carry goes in an Eddie Bauer backpack. That goes almost everywhere...

Meme (2008-03-13 10:05)

Everyone has things they blog about. Everyone has things they don't blog about. Challenge me out of my comfort zone by telling me something I don't blog about, but you'd like to hear about, and I'll write a post about it. Ask for anything: latest movie watched, last book read, political leanings, thoughts on fanfiction, favourite type of underwear, graphic techniques, etc. Repost in your own journal so that we can all learn more about each other.

Meme Answer (2008-03-15 11:48)

This is in response to

puckbunny87 who asked;

> *Name something that gives you an incredible "high" and describe why. (besides your bike, because you already blogged that one ;-))*

I've sat on this question and given it some serious thought over the past couple of days. Mainly because I don't have massively high highs and the flip side of that is that I don't have overwhelmingly low lows either. But there are a few things that make me happy, and give me a real sense of accomplishment when I do them. Here's a list of some as follows:

- Finishing a particularly good book.
- Completing a poem with which I am pleased.
- finding a particular comic book I've been looking for.
- Discovering new music
- Being at a baseball game with my wife. Especially when our team wins.
- Having friends or family over to our house.
- Hearing my nephews laugh or the noise they make when they burst out of the door when we get there.
- Prayer
- Holding my wife's hand.
- And hitting a curve at just the right angle, hitting the throttle and speeding out of it at the right speed on the bike. ;-)

The song "Favorite Things" comes to mind as I write this. It is appropriate to think of these things as giving me a high. Mainly, it's the little things in life that I have learned to appreciate as I get older. Things I was too busy or short-sighted to see when I was younger.

Writer's Block: In this perfect world (2008-03-16 20:32)

LJ Question: What is your idea of a perfect world? Why do you feel this way?

Oh hell, that's easy...a perfect world would be one where the NY Yankees never, ever, ever win another World Series title. Rooting for the Yankees is like rooting for Microsoft or something...

St. Patrick's Day (2008-03-17 20:27)

St. Patrick's Day is usually seen as a chance to knock back beer with green food coloring added, eat corned beef and cabbage and generally go around and pretend you're Irish. I've done this to varying degrees over the years.

One such occasion was back in 1983 (I think). I was a student (ha!) at the local technical school in Green Bay, WI who spent more time making friends and drinking beer than studying. I was having a lot of fun, but not getting much school work done. St. Patrick's Day that year fell on a school day, so the night before was a school night. Funny how things work out that way.

The local hangout at the time was a place on the West Side of Green Bay called The Blarney Stone (or just The Stone to the regulars). They served up beer and whatever else 18-22 year old booze hounds were looking for, and played some fun music to dance to. With a dance floor surrounded by mirrors, it wasn't uncommon for those mirrors to get foggy from dancing fools pounding their feet into bloody stumps acting like we were all that and then some. I should know, as I was one of them.

It was announced a week or so ahead of time that t-shirts would be handed out to the first 50 people to enter the place on the morning of St. Patrick's Day. For some reason, getting one of those shirts became really important to me. So, I devised a plan.

I am a social animal. When I want to do something fun, I like to have people around. This sounded like it had the makings of something fun, so an idea began to take shape. The more people involved, the better. So I thought, so it must be!

There was a large group of regulars that hung out at The Stone, which was always fluid in composition and consumption. Because liquid consumption, hitting on or being hit on was the main attraction. Well, that and the pounding feet into bloody stumps thing. And laughing at others. So, the plan originally was to get to The Stone around 6 am and be first in line. However, it soon became apparent that there were going to be other people who had decided that having one of those shirts was also important to them. Change of plans was in order. So, we did.

One of the the regular things to do was to hit The Stone (or any other watering hold. Lord knows, you couldn't swing a cat in Wisconsin without hitting a tavern, club, bar, or whatever), then go out for breakfast afterwards. It was convenient that an IHOP was nearby (if you call 2 miles nearby) and that was the usual place. Mainly because it was close and who cared about food at 2 am? It was just someplace to go and keep acting silly.

Worked for me.

The new plan was to leave The Stone at closing time, head to the IHOP, chow down, guzzle coffee and kill some time. Which is what we did. Then, we headed back to The Stone to wait. Turns out that the management knew what was going on, and they kindly left the parking lot lights on for us all night long. Which made playing catch with a football or frisbee a lot easier. There had to be around 20-25 people hanging around most of or all night long. It started kind of on the rowdy side (having been fueled prior) and slowly calmed down to just a nice quiet evening/morning of sitting around and shooting the shit about all sorts of nothing in particular. All for a t-shirt. And a chance to hang out in a parking lot all night.

The Stone opened up at 8 am. We all went in, got our shirts, pulled them on over our other shirts and had some green beer for breakfast. Some people stayed through till lunch, some headed home for a nap and class or work. I think I went to school, then home and back to The Stone mid-afternoon. More of the same, don't you know.

St. Patrick's Day has never been quite as much fun or silly since then. I would love to say I got good and hammered, but I didn't. At least, I don't think I did. I don't really remember. Too many beers and years ago…still, it makes for a good memory.

Writer's Block: My favorite memory (2008-03-18 10:46)

LJ Question: What is one of your favorite memories?

That's a toss up. The two most vivid days in my memory are the day I married my lovely wife, nine and a half years ago and the other is the day my daughter was born eighteen years ago next month. Both were emotionally charged and very important to me. Both are fresh and feel like they happened only yesterday. Both were wonderful.

Who Knew? (2008-03-19 11:35)

I bought some CD's recently at The Gates of Hell (read: Wal-Mart) and they were all AC/DC releases. (High Voltage, Highway to Hell, and For Those About to Rock) I listened to a couple of them and ran Back in Black through its paces on iTunes. I was amazed about something.

I was 16 years old, getting ready to turn 17 the year that album came out. I remember the first time I heard, "You Shook Me All Night Long" and just knew it was about sex. It wasn't about love, but it was about sex. Lust and I don't care what your name is sex. And the rest of the album was more of the same. Sex, partying, rock 'n roll. Loud, in your face, with a nod and a wink. Damn, it was good.

I found out later that there were albums released before Back in Black with some guy named Bon Scott singing. It was even rawer and raunchier and just a bit more amusing. I mean, this is the guy who sang the wonderful ode to the plus sized woman in "Whole Lotta Rosie" (that "42-39-56....you could say she's got it all.!.!.!" scream is the stuff of legend). And he died the way he lived. Drinking himself to death. Literally.

I've often wondered what it is about Back in Black that elevated it to classic status. I think I just answered my own question. Primal message, simple sounding sing along songs, and loud....loud, baby, loud!

Age and Old (2008-03-20 16:31)

I've read a couple of things recently here on LJ about people not wanting to be considered "old" or don't think of themselves in that fashion, or just plain don't want to think of themselves as being "old." It's a sentiment I understand, but don't share.

I suppose the reason I don't feel old (although, I joke about it a lot) is that I had a wonderful role model in my maternal grandmother. She lived to be 90 and never really felt old. She gratefully admitted to being older, and realized that she had lived a long time, but didn't associate that with being old. She knew, and so do I, people much younger than I am who are old. It's in their thinking. Their actions and behavior. Mostly, it's in their outlook. They are stuck. Stuck in their thinking. No more decisions need be made. All of life's questions have been answered or ignored completely. Things were "better" in the old days. Which is poppycock, of course.

Things weren't better 50 years ago unless you were a WHITE, male. If you were a woman? Forget about it. In some states, women were still chattel. If you were black? Oh dear lord...do I even need to go into that? Then, there are the so-called deviant lifestyles. Hoo-boy! Were they in for serious problems if anyone found out. Nostalgia in this case is all rose-colored glasses, "Grease" and "Happy Days" reruns.

Things have changed, and there are some things that didn't change for the better. But, that doesn't make all things today bad, just different. So, this old thinking is self delusional at best.

The same pieces I've read had some hope and recognition that you really are as young as you feel. I know young people who have the weight of the world on their shoulders. They feel old and fear getting older. That's such a sad place to be. Breaks my heart, to be honest. I know people over 70 who carry on a bit like kids. The only concession they make to their age is that most of the time, they act it. With a spirit of wonderment and enjoyment.

I guess that's the one thing I really took from my grandmother. It was to never lose that ability to enjoy the world around you. To laugh some. Not only at others, but at yourself. Especially at yourself. Don't spend too much time looking backwards. She had a terrible memory for a lot of past events. Just didn't spend time dwelling on it. She was a marvelous teacher in that regard.

Chronological Age is something we can't really argue with. Becoming old is...

Hello? He's a Jerk, That's Why... (2008-03-21 09:20)

The ever brilliant Don Fehr, leader of the Major League Baseball Players Association, has said they plan on looking into why Barry Bonds hasn't been offered a contract by any of the apparently smarter MLB teams in the off season. Bonds says he wants to play, he's been training and is ready to go.

Clue phone ringing, Mr. Fehr. Here's the answer to your question. Bonds is a grade A, first rate a$$hole. Self-absorbed beyond belief, and has more baggage than a ship's hold, plus there's this pesky perjury thing and the allegations (pretty well proven) of steroid use. Combine that with his churlish demeanor and the fact that he's of little use to a National League team because he's more of a defensive liability than Jose Canseco (which is really saying something) and it's no wonder why the guy has no offers.

I doubt it's collusion, Mr. Fehr. Just an occasional outbreak of common sense amongst the MLB owners. Not usually something you'd think would happen, but there it is...

Writer's Block: Good Catch (2008-03-21 09:31)

LJ Question: Do you have a "catch phrase" for which you are known?

Yes. I saw, "Now What?" a lot. That, and, "Here! Catch!" when I throw something at someone...

> mardeen (2008-03-21 20:49:21) sailed over my head, it did, the first time. Here, Catch! hilarious.
>
> > ying ko 4 (2008-03-21 21:00:09) Subtle, I am...
>
> mysteriouswolf1 (2008-03-22 00:09:28) Haha! Really?
>
> > ying ko 4 (2008-03-22 03:00:24) On occasion, yes. Usually, I'm as subtle as a Mack Truck...

Writer's Block: Stolen Goods (2008-03-24 14:14)

LJ Question: What is the most valuable thing you've ever had stolen from you?

Time. And I've been the thief in the main. Making stupid choices, not following through and just generally being lazy... So yeah, Time...

> mysteriouswolf1 (2008-03-24 19:26:45) I'm sorry about that Mark. That's a very good answer though. And if you want to hear about how my Easter went, just go read my journal...it's under my newest post. :)
>
> ying ko 4 (2008-03-24 19:57:18) Well, who cares about "stuff" that's been stolen. I've got so much "stuff" that I really don't need. Just doing my part to feed the great economic engine, I suppose.
>
> ailado (2008-03-24 21:09:55) Sounds like me. It's a sorry thing, that.

Writer's Block: Neurotic Behavior (2008-03-27 08:53)

LJ Question: What is the one thing you're most neurotic about?

According to that font of all decent and true information, Wikipedia defines neurotic thusly; "*Neurotic*", or *affected by neurosis, has come to describe a person with any degree of depression or anxiety, depressed feelings, lack of emotions, low self-confidence, and/or emotional instability.*

So, if you think I'm gonna spell out all the stuff that I'm whacked about, you're outta your gourd.

I'll cop to two things…and they are quite related. That's seeing CD's outta their cases. If I do, I gotta put them back in. Same goes for DVD's. Which is funny because books and comics and all sorts of crap is strewn all over the house. Much to my wife's chagrin.

Comics and Me (2008-03-27 21:25)

I have never written down how I got into comics. What caused me to become a fan of 4 color fiction. The wonderful escapist and surreal world of long underwear, wish fulfillment, and Archie's terminal problem of Betty or Veronica.

Like most adult comic fans, my own personal "Golden Age" was the mid 1970's. When I was between 10 and 14 years old. Or thereabouts, the memory is a bit foggy at this point. I know I kept them until I was 18 or so, and that for years I sort of regretted getting rid of them. A lot of those old comics have been replaced but they aren't the ones I had, read a few dozen times and loved as only a kid can love.

When my sister and I were little, we lived in Charlotte, NC (with our parents, of course!). There were only a half dozen TV shows that we watched with any regularity. Mother was pretty good about monitoring what we watched, so we watched "Sesame Street", "The Electric Company", "Mr. Rogers Neighborhood", "The CBS Evening News with Walter Cronkite", "Speed Racer" and "Spider-Man"

That's right, the one with the awful animation and the catchy theme song. That's the one. The show I loved as a small boy. I couldn't have been any older than 5 or 6 when that show came on. And the idea of a guy who could climb walls and swing between building was really keen to me. I was so taken with that part that I tried to build my own web shooters. I did it with a plastic cup with a lid, that I poked a hole in the side, managed to get some sort of stick/spindle inside, wind some string on it and there I was. A kid with a cup full of string thinking he was Spider-Man.

We moved at some point when I was 8 or so, and went to Minneapolis. No Spider-Man on TV there that I could find. No Speed Racer for that matter. Did watch some of the old Batman TV show. And to a kid, it was great stuff. Now? I can't watch it. But what these shows did was expose me to the characters. To the concept of Men and Women wearing their underwear on the outside of their long johns and sticking a bath towel in their shirts for a cape and having a lot of fun beating up stupid bad guys. Which is all it was to my young mind at the time.

I discovered comic books quite by accident. I was looking at a magazine rack in a grocery store. I had to be about 9, maybe 10 years old. I didn't really "get" what I was looking at. Until I saw Spider-Man getting pummeled by some guy who was melting. This was happening on top of a subway car, and damned if it didn't look exciting. I'd not forgotten Spider-Man, but I didn't know there was a comic book about him. I was in heaven! I was so excited I bought a Captain America comic book as well! He looked really neat with the shield and wear a flag looking costume. Not as cool as Spidey, but hey! 50 cents later and I was out the door and headed for home. I was a happy kid. I can hardly believe that 2 comics set me back 50 cents.

That just boggles my mind now. I get excited about the Dollar Box at comic shops these days. But, I meander...

The Spider-Man comic that grabbed my attention so dramatically was Amazing Spider-Man 133 and the Molten Man was trying to kill My Hero! Of course, I had no idea who The Molten Man was, but I was going to find out. I read, re-read and read that comic book over and over again. I almost memorized it, I read it so much. I read all the ads, the letter column, Stan's Soapbox, the printing information and couldn't wait for the next issue to come out. I didn't really get that this was the 2nd part of a 2 part story because the writer kindly mentioned what had gone before so I knew all I needed to know to enjoy the comic. That doesn't always happen these days. Then, by studying carefully the editor's notes, I figured out that they were referencing previous issues. So, in this issue, I learned that Spidey had lost Gwen Stacy less than a year before, his best friends father was a nut, and that poor Spidey was wanted by the police. All in 22 pages of amped storytelling. I was in heaven.

The Captain America comic was the concluding chapter of a then huge story line featuring the Secret Empire. I didn't get all the implications at the time, but from my vantage point now, I know that the bad guy was President Nixon and that he was being portrayed as betraying the country in his lust for power. Considering the Watergate scandals going on at the time, this made some sense. Especially when you consider that the writers were young, idealistic kids.

So, this was my introduction to comic books. I quickly found Batman comic books, and since he was depicted as being much more down to earth (no "Old Chum" crap with Robin) and a more serious hero than on the silly TV show, I latched onto him as another favorite. Sadly, to this day, I can't recall what comic I was first exposed to Batman in. Or, The Flash either. I also have to admit that I became interested in characters based on their costumes more than any other reason. I just thought there was something cool about a guy in red long johns with a yellow lightning bolt belt and wings on his head. And he could run fast. What kid didn't dream of doing that? I collected rabidly until I discovered girls, slid the comics to the back of the closet and then traded them later with some kid for some record albums, I think. I came back to comics when I was at a large shopping mall in St. Louis. I'd gone there with my daughter (she was quite young, around 3 or so) to see her Aunt Katie (my sister) who was working her way through school at one of the restaurants in the mall. We ate there, waited for her to get off work by wandering around the mall for awhile. Tony place, this mall. Had an F.A.O. Schwartz toy store, and a Warner Brothers Studio

Store. While there, I picked up a trade paperback of Robin: A Hero Reborn and that created more questions than it answered (Jason who?). So, I went to a local comic shop later and started buying the odd trade paperback, and it spiraled from there. Now, I have prints and Convention sketches, comic strip reprint collections, and more comic books than my wife thinks any grown man should have (she's got a point there...) and hours and hours of reading fun over the years.

So, there's a bit of my comic book collection history. I eventually did reacquire that Spider-Man comic and actually read the first part of that story. But, that's for another day.

My Favorite Authors (2008-03-29 12:20)

This "meme" was snagged with permission from Comicsworthreading.com (which is really worth reading). My favorite authors, and what they taught me about life:

1. Sir Arthur Conan Doyle - The importance of observation. Holmes stated quite often that people see but do not observe. Which means they don't pay attention. Other things I learned was the importance of logic and that there is no such thing as useless knowledge. This, despite what Holmes has said about certain things being of no value to him.
2. L. Frank Baum - An imagination is a wonderful thing.
3. Walter Gibson (writing as Maxwell Grant) - The Shadow Knows! The Weed of Crime Bears Bitter Fruit! Crime Does Not Pay!
4. Stephen R. Donaldson - Learn to forgive yourself. Also, to believe in yourself and others. Finally, that White Gold is cool...
5. Terry Brooks - Sometimes doing your duty is a difficult thing. Doesn't mean it shouldn't be done.
6. J. R. R. Tolkien - Friendship and trust are the most important human qualities. Perseverance is likewise important.
7. Clarence Mulford - Having friends is important. So is a good horse and a six-shooter. Also, Hopalong doesn't really wear black.
8. Van Reid - Never underestimate the power of kindness to one another. Also, the sheer joy of words.

"I'm so amazed" - Mavyn Flyce

These are just a few.

Me, Last.fm and Big Baby Jesus (2008-03-31 16:57)

According to my Last.fm profile, I signed up for and created my profile on that wonderful service back in June of 2006. It's been dutifully tracking what I listen to since then. Well, except for baseball games and irate callers and stuff like that. However, if it's been played on my computer or iPod, it's likely that it's been scrobbled (which sounds vaguely obscene, doesn't it?), tallied and listed.

One of the parts of creating a profile on any of the so-called social communities is a User ID or Screen Name. I have tried to create mine to have significant meaning to me and possibly others. I didn't do either on Last.fm, and I have this silly User Name that generates a few chuckles and questions. Not to mention a bit of head scratching. Why? I had no clue that the rapper lovingly called Ol' Dirty Bastard called himself Big Baby Jesus on occasion. (you can insert an eye roll here if you wish)

So, how did I end up choosing the username? I'll tell ya. It sort of goes like this here...

I belong to the Cardinals ListServ. An email list devoted to discussing the St. Louis Cardinals Baseball Team. The ListServ is owned and operated by ListGod. Not a name he gave himself, but that was bestowed upon him by the members of the List. At least, I hope so. Anyhow, ListGod rides bicycles all over Hell's half acre in Chicago. Which is convenient, because that's where he lives. At least, that's what he says. I mentioned to him that I had an old Peugot bicycle and he was quite excited and also impressed. He asked me to take some pictures, so I did as he requested and created a Flickr account to post them for him to see.

His Flickr account is labeled as "Little Baby Jesus" and I thought that was amusing. So, just to be funny, I named my Flickr account "Big Baby Jesus" which did indeed make him laugh. At least, that's what he said.

On his bolg (he can't spell. Or maybe he can. I don't know) he has some links of interest if you're interested in finding out more about ListGod. I clicked the one that said "What ListGod is listening to" which sounded interesting to me. And it was. It was his Last.fm profile. Seems he's the ListGod there as well. I decided I needed to have a Last.fm account so I could be cool like the ListGod (we'll just call him LG from this point forward. I'm tired of typing out that name) and since I'd just created a Flickr account with a silly name, I did the same with my Last.fm account.

Who knew that there were other people around the world who would pick such a unique and bizarre User Name as I did? Not me. Come to find out that I couldn't use that on LJ. I've wondered if the LG is behind that, but I doubt it. I would have picked his User Name but it does seem to suit him. Besides, he would know who I was and since I knew he'd know, and that he'd know I knew he knew, and this way lies madness, I decided to just punt the whole thing and do something different.

LG has changed his bolg around since then, and his nifty links section is no longer present. At least, it wasn't when I wrote this. He might change it to spite me. He might change it to spite you. He might change it through no fault of your own. Then again, maybe he won't.

LG did like the bike photo's. At least, that's what he told me at the time.

Stars in the Daylight (2008-04-01 14:47)

When my sister and I were growing up, we spent a lot of time with our grandparents. Something for which I am profoundly grateful to our parents for making sure happened. Those were our vacations. While others went to amusement parks or the Grand Canyon, we schlepped off to our grandparents. Which was a good deal as far as I was concerned. My sister agrees. We had wonderful relationships with our grandparents, and our paternal grandmother is still with us. She's 97 and still going strong.

To keep them separated, when talking about and to our paternal grandparents, we called them Grammie and Grandpa. Which suited them. Our maternal grandparents were Grandma and Granddad. This also suited them. All were and remain wonderful people. I feel truly blessed to have been a part of their lives and for them to have been a part of mine.

Grandpa was something of a jokester. Never malicious or mean, but gently funny and amusing. I don't recall what day in April his birthday was, but I know it's written down in my dormant genealogy project. Not that it matters, because we always celebrated or observed his birthday on April 1. Were he still with us, today would be his 99th birthday.

From the time I was around 10 or 11 he started talking to me about seeing stars in the daylight. It was usually during a rainstorm or after dark, or when it was cloudy. The conversation was always short and more of a reminder than anything else. This went on for several years. Always a teasing comment and promise of seeing something amazing. Having a kids attention span, I didn't give it much thought beyond that. And, I knew he was nuts. Nobody could see stars in the daylight in a back yard.

Could they?

I have to tell you a bit about Grammie and Grandpa's house. This was the place where my father had grown up. They had one of the bigger lots in the neighborhood, but that's because they had owned a good part of the neighborhood at one point and sold off pieces of it over the years as the area they lived grew. The backyard was a wonderland to a couple of small kids. There was a path that went to the Grape Arbor. Beyond that was The Shanty. The Shanty was Grandpa's workshop, from which all manner of miraculous goodness came. It had been a chicken house at one point in time, but my father had cleaned it up and set up his Ham Radio outfit in there. When he left home for college, he lost his space to his dad. Seems to me that some of his old Ham equipment was still there, but I don't really know.

The distance between the Grape Arbor and the Shanty was around 20 feet or so. The Grape arbor was a wonderful place. There was a water pipe that came up out of the ground with a spigot where the best water I ever had in memory came from. There was a tin cup that hung from a nail, up high in the arbor, that we drank this water from. It was 4 concrete posts that were around a foot on each side. Hefty posts that held up an equally hefty trellis. On the trellis grew purple grapes that were the center of a weekend every fall. That was because we'd spend the best part of two days picking all the grapes from the vines. Many bushels worth as I recall. Some of them would be eaten immediately, most were turned into jelly by my father and some were frozen. Under the Arbor were two gliders that had been there as long as I could remember. There was also an old metal tractor seat that was affixed to a concrete base, that was buried. I remember asking Grandpa where he got the seat from, and he said it was still attached to the tractor. The whole thing was buried in the back yard and only the seat was exposed. I didn't know any better, so like a trusting idiot child, I believed him. Sort of...

It was a beautiful summers day when the time for me to see Stars in the Daylight arrived. There really wasn't a cloud in the sky and it wasn't at all windy nor too warm. All in all, a perfect weather day for most anything, but especially for seeing Stars in the Daylight. By this time, I'd gotten more than a little curious and had asked my Cousin Bob about it. Apparently, he knew all about seeing Stars in the Daylight and was more than willing to share his exuberance with me, all the while without telling me a damn thing. My Dad assured me that this was something I would long remember, so off to the back yard the four of us trooped. Grandpa, Cousin Bob (who even at that age, everyone knew was going to be a minister. Which he did and is.), Dad and me. The sucker.

I should have known that something wicked was coming this way when I saw the raincoat in my draped over Dad's arm. Why in the heck would anyone need a raincoat on such a glorious gift of a day? Turns out the coat was for putting over my head. Seems it worked just as well as wool over the eyes. It also worked for seeing Stars in the Daylight. Lest you think I'm pulling your leg as hard as mine was pulled, I most certainly did see Stars in the Daylight.

The raincoat was of the London Fog type. Light brown, lots of buttons and a belt around the middle. I have no idea who it belonged to, nor do I care. Suffice it to say, I was put inside the rain coat. Only thing is, they turned it inside out (smell the rat yet?) and it was draped over my head. Dad was kind enough to hold one of the sleeves up so that I could see that lovely blue sky. He's sort of move it around while Grandpa was asking, "Do you see any stars yet?" over and over again. After what seemed like an hour, but was certainly no more than 90 seconds, Grandpa was in the middle of his question when I saw stars. Lots of them.

Remember that tin cup I told you about? While I was being walked (blindly, I might add) down the Garden Path, Cousin Bob (The Minister to Be) was filling said tin cup with enough water to flood the back yard. Okay, so it was maybe 3-4 ounces, but when it came flying down the sleeve of the coat into my face, it seemed like a lot more than it was. Because when that cold water hit my face, as sure as God makes little green apples, I saw stars. Lots of them...

I miss Grandpa and I treasure that story.

Writer's Block: Spring Cleaning (2008-04-03 08:20)

LJ Question: Are you planning on doing any spring cleaning this year? If so, please share a cleaning tip you swear by.

Cleaning? Moi?

Bwa ha ha ha....and if you don't believe me, you can ask my wife!

I used to see signs/posters that read, "A clean desk is a sign of a sick mind" and I believed it. If and when I do clean, I find a trash bag in the left hand useful. When it's full, I'm done. Seldom takes long. Then I sit down until the urge to purge goes away.

Shiny Nothings (2008-04-03 16:10)

<u>Shiny Nothings</u>

My mind works in opening
   lines of poetry
Shiny nickels of verse and rhyme
   tumble about
With nothing to do
   and nowhere to go
It seems the best words come
   when paper is not at hand
As I like awake in
   a restless fugue
A vast panorama goes by
   showing me nothing
The shiny nickels of verse and rhyme
   are nowhere to be found
I hear the tumble in the distance
   or somewhere closer
The opening lines of poetry
   become tarnished and fade.

Writer's Block: The Perfect Crime (2008-04-04 08:57)

LJ Question: What was the last thing you "got away with?"

That's a tough question. I cheated death in a very literal sense. I defeated mine own worst enemy and that was me. I've long done all manner of things to sabotage chances I'd been given, opportunities to better myself or do a job I enjoyed. I allowed foolish hubris to get in the way of a realistic view of myself and my abilities. I finally ended up, not naked in a literal sense, but very much in a figurative sense and I was alone. It really was nobody's fault but mine. Having your faults, mistakes and lousy choices laid bare when you're down and humbled in your own eyes is a hard thing to face. Knowing that I must bear the responsibility for the consequences and not take the easy way out and cling to the victim mentality that is so pervasive in our culture today, was beyond difficult.

I took the words of my Granddad to heart when he told me, "The measure of a man is his ability to admit he made a mistake." That was the first step. Admitting you fucked up isn't the same as doing something about it. And, you can't fix what you won't acknowledge is broken. So, the hard part was doing the admission bit. Hard in the sense that I'd finished breaking myself down to almost raw emotion. Then came the time of healing. It was a spiritual journey and a time of self recognition. I finally learned to accept who I was. I stopped trying to be something I wasn't to impress others. I found comfort in solitude, which told me that I was comfortable in my own skin.

Does this mean that I've licked all my problems? Of course not. I still struggle on a daily basis. There have been emotional casualties along the way. My child, for example. That is something that breaks my heart anew, every day. Sadly, with a stalemate in progress, I can't do anything about it. Except pray and hope.

So, I got away with not doing myself in and giving in to my own horrific self destructive tendencies. I remember the day I turned 25. I saw my mother on that day, and after she wished me a happy birthday, she started to weep a bit. I asked her why she was crying. Her response haunts me to this very day, "I never thought you'd live this long. I thought you would be dead with the way you were destroying yourself."

Self loathing and anger are powerful motivators. They make you think that certain behaviors make sense when they truly don't. They also cheat you out of experiencing the fullness of life that is our gift from God. But mostly, it robs you of yourself. Who you are and what you do with that person. The beauty of it is, you have a choice. You can choose to give in to the lies to yourself (the ultimate victim) or to trust what others have to say. That's what I got away with.

Writer's Block: Saturday Night (2008-04-05 22:23)

LJ Question: How are your Saturday nights different now than they were five years ago?

I go to bed at 10, rather than leaving the house at 10.

That's 10 pm, BTW.

75,000 Miles and a Con (2008-04-06 14:31)

Friday dawned glumpy, overcast and colder than expected. It got little better through the morning. Friday was a vacation day for me, as I had planned on going to Kansas City by way of Jefferson City to visit my friend Eric and his family, and go to the annual Planet Comicon in Overland Park, KS. I was going by way of Jefferson City to get the Gold Wing inspected to satisfy the requirements of government to make sure that my motorcycle was safe enough to endanger my life on for the purposes of obtaining a new sticker on my license plate. That done, I was planning on heading to the Kansas City area on US Highway 50.

So, after riding the 35 miles from our door to Larry's Motor Sport (listening to Sgt. Pepper's Lonely Hearts Club Band on the way), I did indeed get the Gold Wing (injected), inspected, (detected, infected, neglected and selected) and it passed. Never really a concern as I just had some work done on it. I also got a vent for the Tulsa Windshield that I recently purchased used. Come to find out that Tulsa Enterprises no long makes vents for the windshield they sell with a hole in it for a vent. I love capitalism...most of the time.

The nice folks at Larry's found a suitable vent in a new shield that had been sitting around for some time. Long enough that they didn't feel like they should sell it as new, so they pulled the vent out and sold me that one, and installed it for me and everything. I was ready to roll.

I don't think I'd mentioned that the temperature when I left home was 48 degrees. It was still 48 degrees several hours later. Which meant that the blue jeans and two pair of socks I had on under my boots was going to br it. Since a Gold Wing is essentially a Lazy Boy lounger with a huge fairing on the front end, I wasn't terribly concerned. Until I started down Hiway 50 and realized that I had 120 miles to go. This meant when I stopped in California (MO) than I not only needed gas, but to put on my rain pants. This I did, and it's sort of funny to watch people watching you put on pants over your pants in a parking lot. It really must be a sight because people were watching me dress. In public, whilst I already had clothes on. Sort of surreal, I would imagine. Especially in the Mid West where that abnormal sticks out like a sore thumb.

I was set, I was ready and I rolled. West on Highway 50, through towns like Tipton, Sedalia, Warrensburg all the while getting closer to the Kansas City area and the end of my trip. Did I mention that the temperature hadn't changed much? This remained so until I passed Warrensburg. From then on, the clouds parted, the sun came out and the temperature started to climb. To around 57 degrees by the time I reached Lee's Summit. It wasn't a heat wave, but it was warmer than it had been. I hadn't seen many hardy (or dumb) souls out on bikes until I reached the KC area, then there were more and more of them. Amazing what a few degrees does in bringing out the bikes.

My destination reached, I got off the bike, and took my rain pants off in Eric's driveway. The neighbors there, having nothing better to do, watched. People are weird. Unloaded the bike (not much to unload, so it didn't take long) and headed inside. Sat and talked for a spell, went out for dinner to a great German place in Independence (near Truman's home). Eric and I stayed up after his wife and son went to bed to watch "Superman:

Doomsday" but were both so tired we fell asleep while it was on.

Saturday morning arrived and we hit the local Waffle House for breakfast. I was wearing a Mizzou Tigers hoodie and some Kansas Jayhawks fans came in, so we annoyed them, which was fun. Boo Hoo KU! The meal and hijinks concluded, we went back to the house and Eric got ready for his Karate class. He's actually quite accomplished in this and teaches a group of students where he is an instructor at a local college. While he was doing that, I was at the Planet Comicon (or the Con as Eric's wife jokingly and somewhat condescendingly (with tongue planted firmly in cheek) calls it. Eric joined me after taking a few too many shots to the head at Karate.

While there, I spent most of my time in Artist's Alley as the people who create comics are, generally speaking, lots of fun to talk to and watch work. I had my little sketch book and collected a few additions from some of the local creators who were in attendance. I like them because their are in it for love at this point and haven't become jaded. Also, a couple of the artists have and different artistic visions which are great to see.

[Three paragraphs edited out due to heavy reliance on copyrighted graphics]

I grabbed a few comic collections. I snagged two large collections of The Cartoon History of the Universe which is a classic in the field. I remember this stuff from my days as a teen collector. To have it on large collected editions is great. I picked up a Wonder Woman TPB, Capote in Kansas, which is a graphic novel written by Ande Parks. He wrote it about Truman Capote and his time in Kansas doing the work for "In Cold Blood" (which is a fantastic book). He signed it, and got the artist to do the same. I spent some time jawing with B. Clay Moore who writes "Hawaiian Dick" (grapefruit noir) detective stories which make great comics. I bought a collection of one of his other books, and I'm looking forward to reading that as well.

The jewel find was "Mickey Mouse in Color" which is a 20 year old collection of Sunday and Daily strips from the 1930's. All are in color and are considered classic adventure stories. I don't read a lot of Disney, but what I have read, I generally enjoy. Especially the older material. Well written, plotted and drawn, these are just great fun. And this book is nicely put together. And I didn't have to pay full price.

After The Con, we met Eric's wife and son at an Indian place and I had my first go round with Indian cuisine. It was good, but rich. Of course, I like lamb, so that wasn't a big deal. After that, I headed for home. At almost 80 mph, because for all the fun I had been having, I missed my wife. Traffic was light and it was a bit of a different ride home than there because there are no stops on I-70 like there are on US highways that are still 2 lane roads. So, my legs got a bit sore from lack of stretching and the sun was going down on my way home. I had that in my rearview mirrors for a while. Not something I'm used to.

All in all, it was a nice ride, and a good Con (nyah, nyah Sarah). I enjoyed my visit with Eric (and his family, they are all great people). I am quite blessed in that I not only have a great wife, but I really do have marvelous friends. Of course, I always say that I'm not sure if I'm going to go to The Con next year, but I always do...

The 75,000 Miles? Somewhere between The Con and home, the Wing hit and passed 75,000 miles. I missed it...

Writer's Block: Family Matters (2008-04-06 15:31)

LJ Question: What is your "role" in your family?

I don't know that I have much of a role. There isn't any center to the family anymore. I talk to my sister more than anyone else, which is great. I recall a time when I never thought that would be the case. And in my wife's family, since her parents died, there is no center and nobody everyone rallies around. Which is really sad. I miss being a part of a family that is close. Or at least tries to be.

I'm Feelin' Hip and With It (2008-04-09 09:22)

Of course, the younger generation has no frakkin' clue what I'm talking about...lol!

Those crazy folks at the Allmusic Blog released their "Q1 Report: We Pick the Best of 2008 So Far" a few day ago. Last week, in fact. That's how on top of things I am...*sigh*

I'm feeling so 2008 because of the scads of stuff on the list, not only have I heard of at least 33.3 % of it, but I actually BOUGHT 4 releases from this list as well! 4! Now, I suppose you want to know which four, right? Ok....(damn, I'm easy...)

1. Sheryl Crow -Detours
2. Liam Finn -I'll Be Lightning
3. Goldfrapp -Seventh Tree
4. The Raveonettes -Lust Lust Lust (US Bonus Tracks)

Hell of a mix of stuff, right? That's what I'm thinking as I look at it. Still, the one common link is melody. Even with the dissonance in The Raveonettes music, there is a strong underpinning of melody and pop sensibilities. Great stuff, to be honest. The Goldfrapp release is unlike anything else they have released before, but it is assured and confident. Liam Finn shows that while the apple doesn't fall from from the tree (He is Neil Finn's son, after all) he is his own man. Think The Beatles sifted through Elliott Smith and you get the idea. Toss in the pop sensibilities of his Dad and you've got a great record and a great career in the offing. And Sheryl Crow is Sheryl Crow. At least on this album, she pulls in her ambitions and focuses on what she does best and that's crafting solid pop/rock songs. There is a bit of a political bite in some songs, but that's fine. It's not the whole albums worth. Easily her best album in several years.

Grandma's Greeting Cards (2008-04-10 09:50)

Life happens. On a daily basis, we get messes that need to be cleaned up. Sometimes it's nothing more than food wrappers or packaging, others it's diapers or junk falls over. You have to stop and clean it up. All in a day or a life. Just happens.

Yesterday morning was a lovely, albeit chilly, morning. Still, it was more than warm enough for me to ride the Gold Wing to work. I opened the garage door to roll it out and was greeted with a huge pile of "stuff" that decided to follow along. Actually, I think there was a seismic shift and the pile just fell in the middle of the night or something. Anyway, it just flowed out of the garage and into the driveway. Ugh...

It was a box that contained quite a few of the greeting cards my Grandmother had received. She never threw them away. In fact, she joked with us that we would get to deal with it as she had no desire to do so. Usually, this came with a sly grin and a laugh. I miss that laugh...

Here is is, Wednesday morning, the Wing is warming up in the driveway, and I have to clean up this mess of cards. It was something I wanted to do some other time. I knew I'd end up throwing them out, but part of me didn't really want to. It was a part of Grandma, and it was silly, but I knew why I hadn't thrown them out. I couldn't help but thinking at the time that this was Life Happening, telling me to let go and get on with it.

Took about 8 minutes to toss all those cards in a trash can, sweep up a bit of stray flotsam and jetsam and leave for work. I kept thinking about those darn cards off and on all day.

I Got Nothin' (2008-04-15 11:35)

I got nothin'. There is zilch in the cranial cavity that is aching or screaming to get out. Heck, there's bupkes wanting to poke its head out of a bunker and even think about leaving..

sigh*

It was such a crap-o-la morning that if anything was there, the notion went down swirling down the toilets in my head.

Writer's Block: Tax Day (2008-04-15 11:47)

LJ Question: If you're getting one, how are you planning to spend your tax refund?

In a wild orgy of consumer spending madness! I want to do everything I can to kick start the economy, including adding more to the coffers of the exceedingly wealthy in hopes that it will trickle down to the poorest of people in the country! That my spending will singlehandedly make up for the deficit of sales tax income and so forth and so on...

What? You mean it won't work?

Well, fuck that idea...I'm going to put it in the bank. The economy can continue going to hell without me, then...

What is Love? (2008-04-15 20:40)

The word LOVE has caused much happiness and/or misery in most everyone's life. Two sides of the same coin, actually. If you accept the gift of love from someone, they have the power to hurt you. You've let your guard down, shown them your vulnerabilities and trusted them to be kind to you and to those sensibilities. That's a wonderful thing, this gift of love.

What is it, exactly?

Love is confusing, love is frustrating, love is wonderful, love is many things but most importantly love is a verb. It's an action. Think about it for a minute. We all learned the basics of sentence diagramming at some point in our school careers (and if you haven't, you haven't really, well and truly, ~~suffered the torments of academic hell, I~~ mean lived! Yeah...lived!), so if you take the simple declarative sentence, "I Love You" and just look at it for a minute, what's the verb? Where's the action in that sentence? It's not the "I" as that refers to self. It's not the "You" as that refers to another, so what's left? "Love" is all that's left. Love is the action, the verb, the point of the sentence. It's a verb. It's something you do. It's so much more than a feeling.

You want that rush of giddiness? Eat a chocolate bar. It's about the same thing, from a chemical standpoint. Is that love? Nope. Just a spiffy chemical reaction that told you something happened. And that's what a lot of people look at and think love is. A great feeling, a rush of blood to the head, or elsewhere.

Love is something you do. Whether you want to or not, and that's important when you have to make sacrifices for somebody you love. Or when somebody does that for you. You have to recognize them for what they are; Gifts of Love. Don't ever take them for granted. They are precious when freely given. Treat them as such.

Mardeen talked about how she was afraid she wouldn't have enough love for her daughter, which was her 2nd child. I could have told her it was foolish to think such, but that wouldn't have helped her. The advice she got was perfect because it was true. Doing engendered those feelings. The actions of love brought the feeling along with it, and not the other way around.

Love is a verb, so it requires action. I've been most fortunate in my life. I have a wonderful wife who loves freely, openly and every day. She doesn't say it much, unless it's a response to me. She just does it. My Granddad only told me once, in so many words, that he loved me. I never really thought about it, because he did it. He didn't have to tell me, his actions showed me. Loud and clear, in fact. My sister, who I've had a less than stellar relationship over the years, has loved me. In ways I suppose only a family member would know. While I've known at times I wasn't her favorite person, I never doubted that she loved or does love me now. If I were in trouble, she'd be there. Without question.

And that's what I believe love is. An action and belief that when asked, that love will be expressed by being there. Without question.

Is we getting dummer? Does we care? (2008-04-17 09:41)

I am not a college graduate. I am a reformed high school dropout, as a matter of fact. I got my G.E.D. a month or so after I dropped out, and later went back to High School in a different district. Getting my diploma wasn't my priority for that. It was getting a free pass to the Tech School. Graduating from High School was a nice ancillary benefit or a nice side prize. Or so I thought at the time. Having the diploma didn't indicate that I actually knew anything. It indicated to prospective employers that I could finish something I started. That's been the conventional wisdom as long as I can remember. Now, that wisdom has grown to encompass college degrees.

This is a scary, scary proposition to me. What this means to me, is that we as a society no longer place great value on knowledge for its own sake. Knowing just enough to get by or do your job and wallowing in ignorance the rest of the time is okay-fine. Don't the yokels that practice this realize that they are only shooting themselves in the foot? That by being ignorant, remaining ignorant and being PROUD of it, they are turning over the reins of their life to others? That they are no longer participants in what is going on around them because they just don't know?

In a democracy, you have to know what is what, who is who and what's going on with the world around you. How else do you explain the election of a man who doesn't read newspapers? Who knows what he knows and that's all he needs to know? That policy has lead to the insipid and misguided "War on Terror" in Iraq (when Afghanistan should have been our target) and not paying attention to what else was going on. The economy, burning food for fuel in a misguided attempt to reduce our "dependence on furrin' oil" and anyone who ain't with 'em, "hates 'Merica". What rot...and we, as a nation, only have ourselves to blame. Because we not only wallow in our ignorance like a pig in slops, but we celebrate our stupidity. We go on asinine game shows like, "Are You Smarter Than a 5th Grader" and make complete and total asses of ourselves. And we think this is funny! And that this is fine! I watched a few episodes and am amazed at how easy the questions are. There really is no excuse why an adult shouldn't know these things.

Better minds than mine have recently tackled this issue. If you're still reading and not pissed off at me, I highly encourage you to go read the following by [1]Susan Jacoby who wrote a book (The Age of American Unreason) and recently an article in the [2]Washington Post about the Dumbing of America. After that, there is this fascinating article by [3] Kevin Horrigan in the St. Louis Post-Dispatch ([4]"Obama tests America's cult of ignorance") There is also a great [5]article by Patricia Cohen from the NY Times from a couple of months ago about Jacoby's book. They are all worth your time to read and to consider.

I gave my lack of higher education to demonstrate that a college degree doesn't guarantee that you know anything beyond your chosen field, if that. That by reading deeply and widely, you can learn to think, to suss things out for your ownself and not depend on the nattering nabobs of negativity on the TV and Radio "Talk Shows". Further, learn all you can. Knowledge, to this point, is one thing the Government can't tax! Knowledge truly is its own reward.

1. http://www.susanjacoby.com/
2. http://www.washingtonpost.com/wp-dyn/content/article/2008/02/15/AR2008021502901.html
3. http://www.stltoday.com/stltoday/news/columnists.nsf/kevinhorrigan/story/6456113BB260BA35862570540055718F? OpenDocument
4. http://www.stltoday.com/stltoday/news/columnists.nsf/kevinhorrigan/story/48C97E273FFD238986257415005035E5? OpenDocument
5. http://www.nytimes.com/2008/02/14/books/14dumb.html?_r=1&incamp=article_popular_1&oref=slogin
-

R.I.P. Danny Federici (2008-04-18 09:02)

Danny Federici, longtime keyboard player for the E Street Band passed away. He'd lost his fight with melanoma. He was 58.

I'm saddened by this news because Danny Federici was an integral part of the E Street sound. He was also so young. So very young...

I don't really know what else to say. It's not unexpected news, as he bowed out of the current Springsteen tour for health issues...but still...this is just sad, sad news. I've been listening to him play on Springsteen's records for over 30 years. He wasn't one of the flamboyant members of the E Streeters, but this is an outfit where there are no slackers. All are very important to the overall sound of the band. That's probably why most Boss fans prefer his recordings/performances with the E Street Band.

Godspeed, Danny and thanks.

Writer's Block: Outta My Way! (2008-04-18 09:38)

LJ Question: Have you ever experienced road rage?

More when I ride than when I drive. Mainly because I'm so much more exposed on a bike than in a car. And I get to see the stupidity and selfishness of other drivers up close and personal. Cell Phone usage while driving should be outlawed. Not because I think the government should intrude more into out lives, but because it's patently obvious that people, when given enough information, just don't give enough of a damn about other people to shut up and drive. In other words, there is no compelling need for them to hang up the cell phone.

Cage drivers (that would be cars to you non-motorcycle riders) act and drive like they are the only ones on the road. Especially from my perspective behind the handlebars. So yes, I do experience Road Rage. I wanted to shoot a driver through the eyes the other day. Even with a squirt gun, it would have been totally satisfying. Because it was obvious he doesn't use the eyes anyhow...moron...

Book Review: L.A. Confidential by James Ellroy (2008-04-21 21:28)

Writing with an almost brutal style, Ellroy tells a complex story about corruption, obsession, brutality and in a couple of cases, redemption. The main characters are complete and fleshed out, mixed in with historical characters from L.A.'s shady police and government past, Ellroy grabs you from the opening pages and doesn't let you go until the end of the book.

Starting slowly, and painting each character, defining motives for actions and using a brilliant, terse style, Ellroy draws believable people and events on paper with words. The prose hits at times like body blows, jab, jab, jab, roundhouse, flat on the ground, you're breathless trying to keep up. This isn't a book for bathroom reading, too much going on and important plot points can be lost.

Ellroy shows himself to be a master plotter, with few red herrings. He keeps things moving, but the character development is strong.

A terrific book that caused me to lose sleep. I *had* to know what happened next.

[No Title] (2008-04-22 16:45)

Should I go left? (or right?)
Should I stand up? (or sit back down?)
Should I stay? (or should I go?)
Should I do this? (or maybe that?)

Do I fix myself (or rust in this place?)
Do I make a decision (or let inertia win?)
Do I take the chance (or let chance pass by?)
Do I take the leap of faith?
                (or stay rooted in confusion?)

To choose this or that
        is to go through life without fear.
    Fear that rules you
    Fear that controls you
    Fear that Lies to you
        Think you can't when you should
    Fear that cripples you
When you don't decide, the choice
Is made for you. Because that
Decision unmade is truly a decision still.

Should I grow up? (Or stay a child?)
Do I paint this? (Or write about that?)
Does fear defeat me? (Do I Overcome?)

Choose.
    Choose wisely
        Choose Now.

Open Letter to Hilary (2008-04-23 08:59)

Dear Hilary,

Congratulations on your victory in Pennsylvania. You really showed how going in with a 20 point lead and losing 10 of those points is turning the tide, didn't you? Good job.

You have been harping on this notion that you are more "electable" in the fall election than Senator Obama. I got news for you, Senator...not in our house. Not now, possibly not ever. Certainly not at this point in history. I'll tell you why.

We have either had a Bush or a Clinton in the White House since 1989 (Inauguration Day) and I am so not ready for 4 or 8 more years of the same two families being in charge of this country. That would be close to a quarter of a century with two families leading this country. Sorry, not interested. The Bush and Clinton family names are too divisive for that sort of nonsense at this point in time. I want the chance to learn the name of a President with a new last name. It truly is time for a change.

Should you, by some fantastical miracle, win the Democratic nomination, I know that our house will not vote for you. Your pseudo liberalism is as galling as Bush's so-called conservatism. At least McCain believes what he says (when he says it, at least...) and he really is prepared to lead this country in ways you could never be. Obama was right about Iraq, and he is prepared to tell people not what they want to hear, but what they need to hear. I admire that sort of courage. You don't have it. Neither does McCain, for that matter. You are not the solution to the problems this country faces. You don't have what it takes to unite this country. Heck, you're having a hard time uniting your own party!

Do what is right for the Party, for the country and get behind Obama. Get behind pushing the currently led GOP out of Washington. Put your own desires for power and glory aside and truly serve your country. You have such a little chance of winning, nor or in November. All you can do now is cause more dissension and division in not only the Party, but the Country.

Thank you,
Mark

Corner Ghosts (2008-04-23 16:58)

I see these ghosts in
My rear view mirror
Out of the corner of my eye

I saw Tim driving a car
That he never owned
In a place he could not be.

An old man in a fedora
Looked like my Grandfather
Until I looked right at him.

Vaporous memories
That tell me these lies
Out of the corner of my eye

I heard "Roxanne" on the radio
I remember holding your hand
And your heart in mine.

I bumped into Dan in
A corner of my mind
I hadn't seen him in years.

I see these faces in the
Photo album I carry with me
Packed in the attic of memory.

Happy Dance! (2008-04-25 09:07)

I decided that since I am at the point in my life where my cool-ness factor is irrelevant to anyone under 30, I don't care if I look like a doofus and decided to get a *[sarcasm]* Man-Sized Fanny Pack *[/sarcasm]*. So, I did some Google searching and found one that I liked. But, the price wasn't so good. I then decided to look for the [1]same thing at Amazon.com and found it with a price I like better.

So there! The return of the Fanny Pack can't be far behind! (oh, that was a horrid pun...) Would somebody pass the aspirin? I pulled something doing that damned Happy Dance....

1. http://www.amazon.com/gp/product/B000OZE4YE

Writer's Block: Happy Friday (2008-04-25 09:42)

LJ Question: What are you most looking forward to this weekend?

Well, is sure as heck ain't Monday!

Book Review: The Shadow, Volume 7 (The Cobra & The Third Shadow) (2008-04-27 18:00)

"Who knows...what evil...lurks...in the hearts of men?"

The Shadow Knows...

Most people think of The Shadow as a character from an Old Time Radio program that ran for many years during the 30's through the 50's. They would be right.

The Shadow was also a very popular pulp character from the 30's to the end of the 40's. 325 pulp novels were published, most written by Walter Gibson, all published under the Street and Smith house name of Maxwell Grant.

Nostalgic Ventures has been reprinting these fun adventure yarns, along the adventures of Doc Savage, The Man of Bronze. Two yarns to each volume, and not in the original order, these books also have background articles by noted pulp historians Will Murray and Anthony Tollin. They are most assuredly a labor of love and made to last. Nicely done up in a pulp sized trade paperback, these books will be around for a long, long time. Makes reading the original stories easier than trying to track down the expensive pulps.

So, Volume 7 contained two Shadow novels; <u>The Cobra</u> and <u>The Third Shadow</u>. Both written by Gibson and both linked by other characters trying to horn in on the Shadow's game for different purpose's than the Knight of Darkness. Since the stories themselves don't differ all that much in tone, style or writing, I'm going to handle both of them in one shot.

The Shadow lives in a world of black and white. Good guys are good guys and bad guys are downright evil. The Shadow is merciful to those that warrant it, but woe to the evil doer who goes back on his word to The Shadow. There is no nuance in the writing. There are no shades of gray in the tales. Crooks are crooks and they dwell in the "badlands" or "gangland" and are all fair game for the thundering automatics of The Shadow. Justice is swift and sure, as there is no doubt due to the lack of any gray areas.

This Shadow doesn't pal around constantly with Margo Lane (although she does appear in some stories) and doesn't cloud the minds of men. He blends into the shadows of the world around him. Not acknowledged by the police, but tacitly accepted by them, it's a brutal world inhabited by The Shadow and the minions of the badlands.

Character development isn't present in these novels. Purely plot driven, Gibson gives the readers a chance to catch their breath by recapping recent events and hanging a literary arrow to point the way. Bullets fly, bodies drop and in the end, the sibilant laugh of The Shadow shows that *"The Weed of Crime Bears Bitter Fruit...Crime Does Not Pay....The Shadow Knows..."*

Part of the allure for such throwaway fiction is the very disposability of it. It doesn't take itself too seriously, nor should you. It's a dip into a view of the world where the good guys use the methods of the bad guys to ferret them out and dispose of them without fear of mistakes. It wouldn't work in the real world, but one can dream..

Writer's Block: Ghost Story (2008-04-28 08:35)

LJ Question: Do you believe in ghosts? If so, have you ever seen one?

I believe in ghosts. The ghosts of those who have passed and haunt my memories, haunt my dreams, and that I can see clearly out of the corner of my eye. That is, until I look at them straight on. Then they are something else altogether.

I believe in the ghost of a chance. The sliver of a chance that while the world around you is going to shit, somehow...someway, there exists the possibility of making chicken salad out of chicken shit.

As far as actual ghosts that haunt places and such? Casper the Friendly Ghost is about as close to that as I get....

Chick Days (2008-04-29 19:18)

I'd stopped to pick up a couple of sandwiches at the Subway (Eat Fresh!) on the way home. That was to be dinner for me and my lovely bride. Of to the right as I exited the Subway, is an Orcsheln Farm & Home store. Which is exactly what it says it is. There was a large yellow banner across the front of the store (the site of an old Gates of Hell (Wal-Mart)) that read "Chick Days."

This means they have several horse troughs full of baby chickens. Little yellow fuzzy chicks...scads of them. Buy 'em by the bushel, it seems like. And people buy them. In town, mind you. I've no idea what they do with them, but I would imagine that they raise them and eat them or hope for eggs. Whatever, this happens every year. This reminded me of something that happened several years ago. I think I mentioned or alluded to it some time ago, and now is the time to tell the tale.

We live in a split level ranch style home. Built in the early 60's and it comes complete with a mother in law apartment. That's where I lived when I first moved to this address, and when Elaine and I got married. After a while, the people who own the house had to move into town due to school for their kids, and we got to move upstairs. Which left an empty apartment to rent.

I had gone to a particular church for several years, knew many of the people fairly well, and was on good terms with most of them. One of the men in church has a son named Jeff. Jeff is a good kid, who like many people, has made some less than stellar choices in his life. He was really trying to get his life back on track, so I recommended to our landlord (good friends, BTW) that he would be a good renter. Jeff moved in and things seemed set for a while.

Not long afterwards, Jeff's girlfriend Amy moved in. Our landlord wasn't thrilled, to say the least. Can't say that I blame him, to be honest. And Amy was a different sort. a real back to the earth type. She wasn't a hippie so much as just downright weird. Rude as well. Elaine and I weren't overly fond of her. Jeff was fine, but she was a real piece of work.

Within a couple of months, she had dug up a small plot of ground for a garden. Didn't ask anyone, just did it. Then came the first of two dogs. Both Rotweiller's. Big, scary looking, slobbery and LOUD dogs. The first one was Sarge. I forget what happened to him. The second was a puppy named Tank. Tank was big as a puppy, I've no doubt Tank turned into a ginaurmous dog. Tank ended up being turned loose in what was supposed to be our side yard because it was fenced in. We weren't happy with that, either. What happened next should have come as no surprise, yet it did.

One morning I went to take out the trash, and I elected to go out through the side door. I didn't want to carry trash through the house if I didn't have to. I was stunned when I saw a make shift chicken coop in our side yard. Complete with fuzzy little baby chicks. Bought at Orscheln's no doubt. The entire operation appeared out of nowhere, at least to us. When asked, Jeff told us they had been given the baby chicks by a family member and really had no choice but the keep them. Sounded like bull puckey to me, but what are you gonna do? We had free range chickens running around in our side yard.

For some reason the small population of baby chickens declined a chick or two at a time. We figured that neighborhood cats were having dinner on Jeff and Amy, or it was racoon's. The chicks changed from yellow to chicken color, but were still small. Sort of the size of Cornish Game Hens. But they were growing.

One afternoon, I looked in the side yard (we'd accepted that we were stuck with these free range chickens in our yard....we were waiting for the milk goat to show up next, to be honest) and there was Tank, taking a puppy nap. He was tied up in the side yard, and the lead was short enough he wasn't going to get at the ~~snacks~~ chickens in the flimsy chicken coop. The lead holding Tank wasn't very strong either. It didn't take a rocket scientist to figure out what was going to happen eventually.

It took a couple of weeks, but I heard some commotion in the side yard and went to investigate. Inside the chicken coop, looking as pleased as the cat who swallowed the canary, was the puppy who swallowed the chicken. With a little chicken foot sticking out of his mouth. God help me, but I laughed myself silly...more at the stupidity of Jeff and Amy than anything else. We'd told them, but they thought we were full of crap (like the side yard, and dog doo and chicken poo is a horrible mixture when it gets hot...) so they left their big, meat eating puppy in the side yard with a flimsy roll of chicken wire keeping the two apart.

A quick run downstairs to tell them that there dog was eating their chickens, and more guffaws followed. Those poor doomed chickens. Whenever I see that "Chick Days" sign, I think of the big puppy with the chicken foot hanging out of his mouth.

Book Review: The Glasswright's Apprentice by Mindy Klasky (2008-04-29 20:19)

Considered Fantasy, but more alternate reality to my eyes, it's the story of Rani Trader. She's 13 and an apprentice to the Glasswright's Guild in a society built on the Caste System. She ends up being in the wrong place at the wrong time and this begins her whirlwind adventure through this societally constrained world.

The book was fairly well written, and Klasky uses a few unique descriptive phrases and passages. The story is told solely around Rani, there are no cuts to other characters and the behind the scenes machinations. We learn what's going on just as Rani does. It's a very linear story in that regard.

The biggest gripe I had was that everyone around her seemed to know more about what was going on than she did. Since she was supposed to be the heroine of the story, this rang a bit false to me, until I got to the end of the book and realized she was but a buffeted puppet of both sides of the struggle in this story. She did appear at times to be spending more of her time reacting than acting. Then again, she is only 13.

Klasky won accolades for this, her first published novel, and deservedly so. She introduces a fun character in Rani Trader, who has a lot of spunk and spirit, and the less than brilliant decision making of a 13 year old. In short, she rings true as a person. While the writing isn't deft, or brilliant, it is workmanlike and effective at telling the story. And Klasky has a good story to tell. I can overlook the writing lapses (few as they are) for a good story.

If you like fantasy/alternate reality type stories, this would be worth the time. Not the best book I've ever read, but far, far from the worst. I'm on the to 2nd in the series...

Writer's Block: Personality Trait = Trouble (2008-04-30 08:36)

LJ Question: What personality trait has gotten you in the most trouble?

Without a doubt, my temper. I have a wicked temper, and when I get mad all over, it's not a pretty sight. Rational thought takes a vacation (actually, it runs and hides...like anyone with good sense) and I've done things in a fit of pique that have had last repercussions. Couple all that with foolish pride and you have a recipe for disaster.

I do most anything I can to keep control of that temper, and to not take my anger out on those that aren't deserving of it. That's not fair to them, and that's something that I used to do; Blow up at people who did nothing to deserve it.

Ok, politics again... (2008-04-30 15:48)

I'll try and keep this short.

Clinton and McCain both agree that a tax holiday on fuel is a great idea. A wonderful way to help out the average schmuck and beat their chests about "DOING SOMETHING!"

Feh!

It's bull puckey politics, grandstanding and nothing more.

It's also hypocrisy in action as both knotheads are on record as supporting 80 % carbon reduction by 2050. How the hell lowering gas prices is going to do anything but by them some votes with other people's money is beyond me.

Don't be fooled. This is a bad, very bad idea.

Thank you.

Writer's Block: Now I Lay Me Down to Sleep (2008-05-06 15:15)

LJ Question: What is one thing you MUST do before you go to bed at night?

Pee....

Can't Keep Them All (2008-05-08 22:40)

I got too many books. They are everywhere. I got books on shelves, lots of shelves, I've got books in baskets, books in boxes, books in piles, and I'll bet there are some books buried under some green eggs and ham, said Sam I Am...

I've got book in a closet, books in a trunk, books in cabinets, books in drawers (but not with my drawers) and books almost everywhere I look. I never thought the notion of too many books would descend on my home or my life. But it has. I've got too many of them...

What is really troubling is that I've been cleaning out the books for several years now. But no matter how many go out, it seems they are breeding like rabbits or mice when my back is turned because there are more books than there was when I started. And I can't keep them all!

Then...there are too many comic books as well...but that's another subject for another day.

I don't have enough bookshelves".. There, doesn't that feel better? :-)

Book Review: Speed Racer/Mach Go Go Go (2008-05-11 18:08)

A two volume box set reprinting the original manga series as created and drawn by Tatsuo Yoshisa. The packaging is very nice, two hardcover books printed from left to right, in a slip covered box. The art work was restored, or most of it was. There are places where the digital reconstruction wasn't done very well. I'm guessing that was in places that were colored at one point. Most manga is printed in B &W, with only a few pages of color at the beginning of a story, or two tone printing. The first story has some color, then is B &W for the rest of the series. The Japanese covers are included from the 2000 collections as they were originally issued in their native country.

The series itself is a bit different from the TV show as the focus is much more on Speed Racer than the Racer family like the TV show. Their is also more violence than the US viewers remember, as Speed is quite the fighter. Racer X turns out to be working with the police, We see very little of Spritle or Chim-Chim as well. The Americanized names we are all familiar with were retained in this edition. Even though they have little to do with the Japanese version of the same characters. So, while we get the stories as they originally appeared, they have the nostalgic Americanized names. I'd bet it's to capitalize on the Adults who watched the series more than kids today who read manga.

Ah...the stories. What can I say about them? They were created to generate interest in the TV series, and they are middling at best. The art is serviceable, and even recycled in one instance. Seven pages, dialogue and all to be exact! Continuity is not apparent, as the stories just sort of leap about. Racer X comes and goes, get introduced in the same way both times (the recycled pages) and the quality of the stories never rises about adequate. Truly disposable entertainment. Without the phenomenon that is Speed Racer, this series would be forgettable and forgotten. And it's just that phenomenon that makes this collection worth buying and reading, or at least reading. Fun, but not great. Seeing a B level manga from that era alone is worth the cost of admission as most manga that comes over here is the cream of the crop. There is so much that we just don't see, and that's probably a good thing.

Writer's Block: Where am I in the garden? (2008-05-13 08:19)

LJ Question: What vegetable or fruit do you relate to most?

I'm a tomato. Tomatoes come in all shapes and sizes, mostly round. Some are longer than others, some are more wrinkled and then there are the cherry and grape tomatoes. Lots of room for identity problems in being a tomato. Room for diversity in being a tomato.

Did you know that calling a woman a tomato can be a good thing? You can look it up! It's also a slang term for a stupid person. You can look that up as well. Such a useful word and a useful plant. I love tomatoes, but am not fond of ketchup. Spaghetti sauce made from tomatoes is divine (HA!!) and tomatoes are wonderful in salads.

Tomatoes are basic, simple and prevalent. Most anyone can grow a tomato, most everyone likes tomatoes. I like being a tomato. And when I wear a large red sweatshirt, I feel like a tomato. Which is why I'm trying to lose weight....

Writer's Block: Remembering mom (2008-05-13 22:57)

LJ Question: What's your favorite memory of your mother?

I doubt this qualifies as my favorite memory. It is, however, a lasting one.

Some years ago, probably close to 20 or so, I was working at a radio station in Boonville, MO and my mother was living and working in Marshall, MO. About an hours drive away to the west. Not a trip I made a lot, but often enough over the years.

Mother was a practicing psychologist. She'd gotten her Master's Degree and went to work for the State of Missouri. She liked her job and was pretty good at it. She also had the unnerving habit of playing therapist with the family. Whether they participated or not, that was the case. She could explain why everyone was the way they were. Or at least how she saw things in that regard.

I was fortunate. I was given special treatment. I got TOLD what my problems were. Somehow, she was never at fault. This didn't dawn on me until years later, but not at that time. She was good at noticing things, and realizing that I was hurting a lot at the time. In a lot of emotional pain, to be honest about it. I was the problem child. I freely admit that. Caused all sorts of problems for my parents. I lived in "interesting times" and had a...unique...set of parents. They were not well matched. However, they don't test for that or make people get licenses to be parents so you make do with what you have.

This particular visit was emotionally draining. I know now that my mother meant well. At least, I hope the hell she did. Because she inflicted a serious hurting on me that day. It went a little like this...

She'd just moved in to her place a month or so ago. Nice apartment and I was there to hang pictures, hook up her stereo, and general Son stuff. Help out your mother kind of stuff. I got fed, and the food was always good so it was a win-win situation. After the stereo got hooked up, out came mother's records and tapes. We had a lot of the same taste in music (and some that was not at all the same) so she put on a record and we ate and talked and seemed to be having a good time. After a while, the Neil Diamond came out. Neil Diamond is one of two artists I strongly associate with my mother. The other is Tom Jones. He has nothing to do with this story...

Mother put on the Diamond album (Greatest Hits, if memory serves) and when a particular song come on, she asked me to be quiet and listen intently to the lyrics. Ok...I can do that. And I was fine until the chorus came around;

"I am," I said
To no one there
And no one heard at all
Not even the chair
"I am," I cried
"I am," said I
And I am lost, and
I can't even say why
Leavin' me lonely still

Which pretty well summed up how I felt about life at the time. And mother knew it. It felt like a body blow. I could almost literally feel the air rush out of my lungs, my confidence seemed to dribble down my leg and puddle on the floor. I felt like a little boy who had just wet the bed (again...). I felt naked and exposed. I felt betrayed.

I felt alone.

Mother brought this to my attention, but offered no way for me to deal with it. I had these issues, I felt isolated and alone. Thanks for pointing this out, Mother...but now what the fuck do I do?

No practical answer that I can recall.

I went slinking home to my little hovel in Boonville. It was a lonely drive. The pain had been brought out into the open. I had to deal with it somehow, so I started drinking a lot again. Self-medication was always a specialty of mine. I was good at numbing the pain through "medicinal" hooch. I used it as as excuse for bad behavior. I used it as an excuse to avoid dealing with the issues that caused the pain. I ran away and tried to hide from myself. However, when I woke up all hung, flung and slung the next morning, I was still there. I couldn't get away from me.

I can listen to that song now and think to myself that it's a song of a very lonely man. I know I'm not that person anymore, but those feelings took some time to deal with and get past. I also wonder if that was my mother trying to tell me something about her. In a Freudian way, of course...

Happy Mother's Day, Mother. Wherever you are, and sorry it's late...

Writer's Block: Three dishes I could live on (2008-05-15 10:26)

LJ Question: What three dishes could you live on for the rest of your life?

The temptation to put a snarky answer such as A dinner plate, a soup bowl and a sandwich plate is overcome by the idea that a food post that doesn't mention bacon, in all of its bacony goodness would be a real waste.

So, with the sound of bacon frying in my mind, and the idea in my head (and the phantom taste on my tongue), I offer these are three "dishes" I could live on/with for the rest of my life....

Bacon and Eggs (with toast and jam/jelly/peanut butter), oranges, steaming mugs of coffee and the occasional bowl of oatmeal. Pancakes and eggs w/Bacon. Preferably from the Cracker Barrel as their bacon is divine.

And the last "dish" is my wife. She's the "dish" for me! Did you know that [1]Bacon Is a Vegetable? It's True! [2]You can even buy a t-shirt that says so!

1. http://dieselsweeties.com/archive.php?s=931
2. http://www.dieselsweeties.com/shirts/baconisavegetable/

Ode to Bacon (2008-05-15 16:14)

I've had bacon on the brain today. No real reason, just craving some bacon. Which is strange, because I had bacon the other day...

So, in honor of today's obsession, I present this little ode to pork fat.

Encrusted in pepper
Injected with syrup
Hung so the smoke from some
Hickory will add to
The flavor already divine

If you cook it too fast
It will burn, become brittle
Slow, over low heat
Is the way you should go

You can't rush perfection
For sandwich or breakfast
So plan ahead carefully and
You'll soon see why T
hat everything is better
With bacon to fry...

This Pear (2008-05-16 15:19)

I've a cold pear sitting on my desk
It's not doing anything, this pear.
Just sitting on my desk.

It is green, this pear.
With flecks of brown,
       cuts, nicks, scrapes, this pear.
Hardly perfect in appearance, this pear.

Lopsided, dimpled,
Hiding a sweetness within
Revealed in the first bite
       of this pear.
Thick green skin gives way
To juicy flesh, this pear does
Frothy dribbles down the side, this pear.
Ravenously devoured to the core, this pear.

Not lovely like the apple, this pear.
Still, conveys a comfort And joy, this pear.
And now...it's gone. That pear...

Book Review: Shades of Glory -The Negro Leagues and the Story of African-American Baseball (2008-05-26 20:08)

<u>Shades of Glory: The Negro Leagues and the Story of African-American Baseball</u> by Lawrence D. Hogan

Purporting itself as "the" authoritative history of Black Baseball, this book fails at that. Quite simply because to do that in the space allotted to this book would be impossible. Too much history, too many people, teams and games for the complete tale to be told. Which is where this book fails ultimately. Too much story, not enough space to flesh it out.

Hogan attempts to start at the beginning of Black Baseball and go forward, but all he can accomplish is a cursory glance at best, and listing of facts at worst. The writing is uneven with some parts well done and others just shamble along, looking for something interesting to grab onto.

There also isn't enough background information about the Black Experience to put the entire story in context. Some is, but as it is more a story of people, more stories about people rather than organizations would have been more desirable to me.

This is an admirable undertaking, and one worth doing. That Hogan is passionate about the subject matter is undeniable, that he knows it backwards and forwards is also without question. However, the ways in which he tries to convey this leaves the reader cold. More storytelling and less fact listing. As it was, I was unable to finish the book. Reading it became a chore, and this pains me to say. Baseball, and Black Baseball in particular are subjects I enjoy, so I was predisposed to really like this book.

A complimentary copy of this book was provided by the Publisher.

Writer's Block: Perfect Sandwich (2008-05-27 21:53)

We just got back from a trip to Ohio to visit family and friends. While in Toledo, we went to one of our favorite haunts, Schmucker's Good Food. I had a Dagwood Sandwich from their menu. It consisted of three pieces of Rye bread (my favorite), and on one section was Hot Ham and Cheese, and the other layer had a fried egg, cheese, lettuce, tomato and it was supposed to have mayo, but since I'm watching what I eat, I passed on that. ;-) (I don't like mayo on sandwiches...)

That was about as good a sandwich as I've had in some time. Except for peanut butter, whether with jelly, cheese, baloney, honey, butter or by itself...peanut butter sammiches are the best!

Schmaltz-a-Go-Go (2008-05-29 09:35)

Oy! Has it been a depressing past couple of days from a musical standpoint. I looked at my Last.fm plays from the past couple of days and I have to wonder if I am in my right mind. I mean, yesterday I listened to an entire Carpenters album. Today, it's a Frankie Valli and the Four Seasons collection. Now...now I am listening to AM Gold CD's. Such serious fare as Edward Bear's "Last Song" Sweet's "Little Willie" and upcoming in the hour is Ray Steven's happy shiny ode, "Everything is Beautiful" complete with hokey children's choir.

Man, I've turned into a sap...what next? A Neil Sedaka marathon?

Singin' to the Radio (2008-05-29 15:07)

This is something lots of people do in the privacy of their own cars. I've done it for years...mainly with the windows up so I don't get arrested or shot. Or both...

However, I have found myself singing along to the radio whilst riding on the Gold Wing. There ain't no doors on that thing, nor any windows...

Fortunately, nobody has thrown anything at me.

Yet..

Neil Young (2008-05-30 08:45)

Neil Young, for me, has always been just one of those artists that I liked to listen to on the radio. I never really had the urge to buy anything that he recorded. Heck, I didn't even bother to download any of his music. If I really wanted to hear something by him, just turn on the radio and wait an hour. Guaranteed that something by him would come along. In the past 30 years, I've only bought one recording by him, and that was "Freedom" solely for that rock-tastic, angry title track (angriest, most pointed protest song I've ever heard. Visceral in its seething, palpable anger. It is a musical body blow). I listened to the rest of the album a few times, but put it away and only ever got it out to add the one song to a mix tape or CD.

That changed recently. I ran across a copy of Decade, which is now almost 30 years old, in the used bins at the local record store. I didn't even listen to the whole thing in one day, as is my wont with new CD's. However, I would listen to bits and pieces and found myself drawn more and more into his musical web. Songs that were long familiar were now fresh and new, somehow. Like I had gained a deeper appreciation for them and had found more enjoyment from them.

So, Neil Young has gone in my world from the guy with a weird voice, to that guy with interesting things to say and a unique and varied way of saying them.

So, Our Trip... (2008-05-30 21:17)

Recently, on a Wednesday not long ago, my long suffering wife (she IS married to me, after all) and I got our tired bums out of bed at the indecent hour of 5:00 am. That's in the morning, Boys and Girls. Before Breakfast early...the chickens were still sleeping. At least, I assume they were as there aren't any more living around the house these days.

Why, would two otherwise rational adult human beings get out of bed so early in the middle of the week? It's not like we were going to go garage sale-ing or anything like that. No, we got up that early to load up the mini-van with "our stuff" await our dear friends, Pat and Sheila (the same Sheila who did the marvelous painting I posted a couple of days ago) to arrive, load "their stuff" into the same van and head off to see my paternal Grandmother. Grandma is 97 years old, and lives in Toledo, Ohio (cultural center of the upper midwest! LOL!), where my father was born and raised. My aunt still lives in the area as well.

Driving from Central Missouri, we ventured to Auburn, Indiana to stay that night. A night spent in a Days Inn, followed by what passes for a "free" breakfast the next morning, and we headed to the Auburn Cord Duesenberg Museum. Elaine and I had gone there several years ago, and I just knew that if the chance presented itself, I had to take Pat there. Auburn's, Cord's and Duesenberg's are quite simply some of the most beautiful cars ever built. And they were built for the most part right there in Auburn, Indiana. We really enjoyed our time there, and before we left town we stopped in to take a gander at the NATMUS (National Automotive and Truck Museum of the United States) museum directly behind the ACD Museum. While the ACD museum took more than 2 hours to see most everything, NATMUS took less time than it does to say their full name. A couple of interesting things about it were all the International Trucks in the basement, and a few of the cars on display were actually for sale. Including a 1976 Gold Wing in pretty good shape for a bike that old. Still, ACD was well worth the time and NATMUS? Not so much.

From there, we continued up I-69 to the point where it meets up with I-80/I-90, otherwise known as the Indiana Toll Road. This is in the area of Fremont, IN and there is an Outlet Shopping Mall located there, amongst the truck stops, choke and pukes, gas stations and fireworks stands. There are only two stores we bother to stop and look in anymore. One is Socks Galore. Elaine is a socks fiend. She still has socks from her days in Jr. High School. Since I have comic books that old or older, I point no fingers nor poke any fun (ok, so I do a little...what the heck, right?). The other is a pickle place named Sechler's. Any place that can make pickles called Candied Orange Dill Pickles (or something like that) gets not only a tip of the hat, but a bit of the money in my billfold as well. They make great pickles and wonderful relish. We bought a few jars, and headed off to lunch. It was, after all, past lunch time by this time and the pseudo free breakfast from several hours ago had worn off.

When in the area, another place we frequent is Clay's Family Restaurant. Nobody named Clay has owned the place since the mid 70's, but when the people who own it now bought it then, it had been Clay's for 25 years. They figured that no matter what they named it, people would refer to it as Clay's for around 10 years, so why bother? I like that sort of thinking, and we love the food. It's not far from Lake George, and we can see part of it from the window seat we always try to get. We had a fairly light lunch because we were only an hour or so from Toledo and that dinner wasn't too far off in the distance. Still, we enjoyed our lunch and I had a piece of their Rap-apple-berry pie (don't ask, just try some) then took to looking at the for sale decorations on the walls. Local artists sell paintings, photo's and such. It makes for a nice variety between visits and cheap decorations for the place.

Funny story about another visit to Clay's. We were sitting down, munching away on our lunch and this lady who had sat down behind us asked me what was good on the menu. We told her a couple of things we both liked, and we started talking to her a bit. Turns out that she owns a local place of business (here in Columbia) with her husband. I pass this place every day on my way to work, as it happens. She lives in St. Louis where they have another store by the same name. It just goes to show you that we do, indeed, live in a small world. Every so often, as I pass the place on my way to work, I think of that incident and Clay's.

When we got to the hotel located across the street from Grandma's home (she lives in a marvelous facility that allows independent living with some help if needed), there was a drug bust being finished up in the parking lot. Nobody at the hotel knew anything, so I went and asked to police. They were only too happy to tell me all about it. Main reason I asked was I was wondering if it was safe, you know? Anyhow, Toledo's finest assured me we were quite safe, so we unloaded the mini-van, freshened up and went over to Grandma's.

When we got there, I was pleasantly surprised to see my Aunt, her husband (Bob Honey) and my dad. Actually, Dad being there wasn't such a surprise. He phoned on Tuesday telling me he would be there. However, I didn't expect a houseful to add to the houseful we brought with us. I can just imagine how pleased Grandma was having so many family and friends close by and in her home that afternoon. Family is very important to her, and she loves having them around. We were all quite pleased to be there.

I wasn't expecting to see Aunt Vi and Bob Honey as we were told they were going to be out of town. However, they were leaving early the next morning, so they came with Dad and we all got to see them and they got to see us! That worked out quite well, all the way around. Dinner that night was at Al Smith's Place, an eatery up the road from Grandma's. The food is good, if not spectacular. Except for the Bread Pudding, that is. It is quite simply to die for. Were I too be executed tomorrow, I'd want that on my dinner plate for my last meal. It's that good...and Pat and Sheila thought so as well.

I had the pleasure of Grandma sitting to my right and Elaine to my left for dinner (and most meals where we all were together), chatting and talking quietly while the rest of them were having their own conversations. She is such a dear lady to me. I can't begin to explain how truly blessed I feel, having her and my other Grandmother for Grandparents. They are as different as night and day, but terrific women, mothers and people for all that. I know my life is better for knowing them both.

Anyhow, after a lot of shenanigans at Al Smith's, the party broke up, hugs all around and we went with Grandma back to her place for a bit. I made arrangements to meet Dad for breakfast the next morning and shortly after that, everyone went to bed.

I got up quite early the next morning, as did Elaine. We both were going to join Dad for breakfast, but she told me that getting ready wore her out, so she went back to bed and I sallied forth with the Olde Man. Aunt Vi and Bob Honey told him of a place to try for breakfast and we found the Sylvania Diner without any trouble. Mainly because it was right where Bob Honey said it would be. It has all the visual charm of a carpet store, to be honest. The food and service? Amazing.

Imagine an omelet stuffed with a gyro for breakfast. That's pretty much what my dad had. I went the skillet route and had eggs, fried potatoes, grilled onions and peppers and gyro meat. Outstanding. Simply amazing food. Oh, was it good. It was so good that I dragged everyone back for dinner that Friday night. I tried Falafel's for the first time and they were amazingly good. Everyone enjoyed the dinner. And the guy who let us in the place early that morning was still there that night. He wondered if we were going to move because we liked the food so much!

Between breakfast and dinner, the four of us went to Ann Arbor, MI. It's where I grew up and it's about 45 miles north of Toledo. Here ends part 1 of the story...

My Toenails... (2008-05-30 22:53)

Since somebody (who shall remain nameless) said they could read about this....(see comments in previous post)

It was a dark and stormy night. By candlelight, because all the lights had gone out due to said storm and it being dark out, I decided that since I couldn't see well enough to read (the name not being Lincoln), I fished around for my Male Pedicure Kit. Said kit consists of two nail clippers (large and not so large), a metal file (no emory boards for REAL men), a tweezer that's mainly for show and pulling slivers out of manly calloused hands (or feet if they are ever sandaled rather than shod) and for some unknown reason, a dull knife with a bottle opener in the handle.

After casting about for a moment, I found the object of my hunt, opened the case to make ready my tools for the task at hand...took off my shoes and socks (Note to self: Odor Eaters) and clipped my toenails. When I was done, I gathered up the leavings as best I could, dumped them in the trash, and then Voila! The lights came back on!

I went to bed after that.

Writer's Block: The Only True Question: (2008-05-30 23:13)

LJ Question:
If you could go back and fix your most regrettable decision, what would it be, and what would you do differently?

Or:

Pirates or Ninjas?

Neither, actually. Pirates have been dwelling in the cellar of the NL Central for so long, they own it. And Ninjas are crotch rocket type motorcycles. They look great, I like the design and they go like hell. They also look uncomfortable as all get out for guys with Dunlop's Disease (go google it, already...)

Writer's Block: Fixing the past. (2008-06-01 18:58)

LJ Question: If you could go back and fix your most regrettable decision, what would it be, and what would you do differently?

Or:

Pirates or Ninjas?

I would have fought with my ex-wife over visitation with my daughter. I would have called her bluff, and stood up to her. I would have swallowed my foolish, stupid pride and got in her face. I would have ultimately made our daughter a victim, but she is anyway so what difference does it make in the final analysis? At least, I wouldn't loathe Father's Day and have the failure of one of the greatest joys and responsibilities G*d grants us thrown in my face every year for a month on TV. It's not enough that I live with the guilt, remorse, anguish and knowledge she may never, ever speak to me every day. That the only memories I will carry with me of her end when she was 6 years old, and that the most recent photograph I have of her is her kindergarten picture. No, I live with this every day. I lose sleep. My fault...

I live with this hole in me every day. Most people never see it, because I choose not to share it with them. It is my biggest failure, my hugest mistake. It's beyond regrettable, it's awful. By doing nothing, she feels abandoned and rightly so. Most anything I do now has to ring hollow. Again, my fault...

If I could go back, my daughter still might not want much to do with me, but at least she'd know me. Know who I am, know who the rest of her family is, and could make informed choices rather than purely emotional ones. At least she'd know...and now she doesn't.

I'm so sorry, Dear Daughter.

The Trip, Part the Second... (2008-06-05 07:18)

Where were we...oh yes. Between breakfast and dinner on a Friday on our recent trip.

After a fine and dandy breakfast with The Olde Man (a term of love, respect, affection and endearment), everyone else was rousted and ready to go. Go where? Ann Arbor, MI where I grew up way back when. When we moved there, it wasn't long until Jimmy Hoffa went missing. This is a perfect example of correlation not meaning causation.

I made sure that everyone else had some breakfast, I got some coffee (all accomplished at [1]Tim Horton's), we got some gas, and headed up the roads I had traveled so many times when I was a boy. Those roads that went from Toledo, OH to Ann Arbor, MI along US Highway 23. As we got closer, memories washed over me like rainfall. Bits, flecks and flashes of people, places and things. All crowding around, some demanding attention and some just waving on their way through. Familiar street names, and buildings. Places I'd never seen before and the like. It was so familiar and strange at the same time. We exited at Washtenaw Ave and headed into town. Most all of the business's that were there when we lived there we gone, but the buildings looked familiar. Except for the one stretch. Nothing was the same. Then again, nothing is the same, so it doesn't really make much difference. Except for the Arby's (still has the same old fashioned sign), nothing was where it should be. Including me. This isn't home anymore. Hasn't been for many years. Still, it was nice to be back.

We make it to downtown Ann Arbor, park in a garage I never had to use before. I never drove in Ann Arbor. I got my license in WI when I was 17, so I rode a bike all over hell's half acre. Almost literally. I put over 1,000 miles a summer on my bicycle as a kid. And I never went much of anywhere. Just went.

We first went though the [2]Nickel's Arcade. Lots of interesting stores and what not. One of the place I remember was this funky, dark old Tobacco Shop called Maison Edwards. I never bought anything there when I was a kid, but I did step inside every so often for a free smell. Old tobacco shops always smell so good. Very male, almost. Sort of a sanctuary, you could say. I would imagine hard boiled types buying their cheap cigarettes in a place like that, then a few minutes later, an academic with fastidious tastes buying his oh so perfect pipe tobacco. I bought a new shaving brush, some bay rum shaving soap and a bar of Italian soap that smells like a tree. All in all, a Manly Man's haul. Pat looked at buying a straight razor and strop. He took a business card, and we both left.

For the next couple of hours, we essentially wandered around the downtown area that I remembered. Some places were still there, some weren't. Just a fact of life. I did see the marvelous [3]State Theater where I saw Young Frankenstein. Man, that is a lovely theater. The Michigan Theater is also still around, but I don't really remember it all that well. I'm sure I went to movies there, but none stick out. We went to the old neighborhood, which is a nice neighborhood. But, I noticed it's aging. There were signs such as paint that needed scraping and reapplying, and a couple of yards weren't as neatly trimmed as I remember. And there were no kids running around anywhere. It was so quiet. No traffic to speak of. It wasn't a loud neighborhood by any stretch, but it showed signs of life. Not this time. It also seems smaller than it did when I was a boy. The streets are shorter, the houses closer together and smaller. Perspective being what it is, I'm sure the years have done their number on the memories. That, and I don't walk the place anymore. Or ride a bike....

We went to my friend Brian's home. Actually, it's the home of his parents whom I adore. Karen and Max are delightful people who have always made us feel welcome in their home. Karen and Max took us to lunch at The Gandy Dancer. It's in the old train depot and has been there for as long as I can remember. Incidentally, it's the place I first had lobster. That was almost 30 years ago...

Lunch was filled with many laughs, shared stories and enjoyable food. I consider it to be time well spent. Pat regaled us with tales and Karen asked many questions, as is her wont. She likes to know. And I find that admirable, to be truthful. Max told a few tales as well, and well all clapped enthusiastically when a passenger train passed by. That is the custom at the Gandy Dancer, after all.

It was getting late in the afternoon, so we headed back to Toledo after taking out leave of Karen and Max. We had planned on stopping at a Cabela's located along Highway 23, but time got away from us. Pat was sorely disappointed and I feel bad about it even yet. However, we made it back to Grandma's, and after a bit of getting ourselves back together, went back to the Sylvania Diner where we had a wonderful dinner.

Saturday we slept in a bit. Got a later start and walked to a nearby eatery for breakfast. We visited with Grandma for a while, then the whole lot of us went to Schmucker's Good Food for lunch. They have marvelous pie. I had Rhubarb and so did Grandma. Elaine had Coconut Cream and Pat and Sheila split a piece of Apple Pie.

The rest of the afternoon was spent just visiting. Listening to Grandma tell a few stories and sharing recollections. Hearing her talk about the soldiers marching off to World War I down High Street in Columbus, and the constant changing of schools due to the flu epidemic in 1918 was riveting. We all got a point of view that a history book just can't impart. I really wish I'd taken along a tape recorder. Some tapes to go with the growing accumulation of letters would be a wonderful thing years from now.

We went to dinner at [4]Tony Packo's (Grandma elected not to join us). There are a few locations around Toledo, but we went to the original location. The one Klinger talked about on M*A*S*H. It's a real place, and the atmosphere is amazing. There are buns all over the walls that have been autographed and mounted in cases with a small plate underneath telling you who signed it. Makes for an interesting activity looking at who has signed what. And the food is marvelous. I'm so glad we don't live closer. I would weigh 900 pounds in a New York Minute,

I'm afraid. We spent an enjoyable evening with Grandma, and had some of my Aunt's wonderful Cherry Dump Cake. In looking back, it seems all we did was eat. And that's partially true. We did spend a lot of time around a table. But there was always great conversation and lots of laughs.

Leaving Grandma seemed harder this time than other times. She got a bit emotional, which isn't the norm. Then again, she is quite aware of her mortality. She really wants to make it to 100 years of age. She wants to vote this fall to oust the Republicans, and both are major goals. I think that these goals have helped her to live as long as she has. She spends time following the news as best she can. But she knows her days are fewer and fewer. She shares more and more of herself with each visit. Parts I never knew or thought about. So, it gets harder for the both of us each time. Harder for Elaine as well. Those two are so attached, and so close. It's been wonderful watching those two bond like they have. Sharing two such special people with each other has been a special privilege for me. Sharing Grandma with Pat and Sheila and the other way around was also a special thing. She has made them welcome and I hope they return with us. They are great friends, and very special people. Pat was Best Man at our Wedding and Sheila was in Elaine's Bridal Party. There is Family you're born with and Family you choose. Pat and Sheila fall into the latter category.

The trip home was fairly uneventful. Except for the heavy rain in Southern Illinois and the A/C being dead, that is. Other than that, we made it home in jig time and plenty of daylight left. It was a great trip and next on our travel agenda is New York City later this summer!

1. http://www.timhortons.com/
2. http://www.leeandkristin.net/AnnArbor/Downtown/Arcade1.html
3. http://michtheater.org/state_about.php
4. http://www.tonypackos.com/index.php

Totally Random (2008-06-05 19:49)

I don't know if you've noticed, but there is a new link across the top. You can now click the Random Journal button and go wherever LJ takes you...

So, I did. And all I found were LJ's written in Russian, or other languages I don't read...the only one written in English was written in Teenage Girl English. A bizarre dialect I just don't understand....

And Rupert Murdoch is one of the ugliest human beings alive.

Last Three Months (2008-06-11 07:55)

1	She & Him	157
2	Frank Sinatra	152
3	Duffy	149
4	Paul McCartney	147
5	Neil Diamond	135
6	Counting Crows	116
7	Bruce Springsteen	113
8	U2	110
9	Michael McCuistion	110
10	Tommy Tutone	107

If anyone really cares, here's what Last.fm says the Top 10 artists (with number of tracks played) from my charts for the last 3 months. Helluva combination, huh?

Born To Run (2008-06-12 09:56)

Yesterday, "somebody" (who shall remain nameless) made the comment that they didn't like Springsteen's voice. Fair enough. However, coming to the defense of goodness and light, herrgooch made the comment that there is a distinction between his writing voice and his singing voice. Very true, and not something I'd really given much thought to before.

Here are the lyrics to "Born to Run" which is quite possibly, the perfect rock 'n roll song written in the last 40 years. Words in italics are my thoughts on the lyrics and bring a focus to Springsteen's writing voice.

In the day we sweat it out in the streets of a runaway American dream (working)
At night we ride through mansions of glory in suicide machines (cruising, relaxing, dreaming) Sprung from cages out on highway 9, Chrome wheeled, fuel injected and steppin' out over the line (pushing our luck)
Baby this town rips the bones from your back (town is dying, sucks the life out of you)
Its a death trap, its a suicide rap (more than your body will die here, dreams/soul/hope)
We gotta get out while were young (something better over the next hill) ' cause tramps like us, baby we were born to run (There's Hope in the distance/future)

Wendy let me in I wanna be your friend I want to guard your dreams and visions (trust me, we'll face this together)
Just wrap your legs round these velvet rims And strap your hands across my engines Together we could break this trap (we can't do it alone)
We'll run till we drop, baby we'll never go back (Hope, slim and fleeting, but it's there)
Will you walk with me out on the wire 'cause baby I'm just a scared and lonely rider (I'm as alone in this as you are)
But I gotta find out how it feels I want to know if love is wild, girl I want to know if love is real (is it more than a dream? is it more than fleeting?)
Beyond the palace Hemi-powered drones scream down the boulevard (taking life in their hands) The girls comb their hair in rearview mirrors And the boys try to look so hard (to stare down the darkness in their own life)
The amusement park rises bold and stark (a place of fun, is actually a reminder of grim reality) Kids are huddled on the beach in a mist (looking tough, but really scared underneath it all)
I wanna die with you Wendy on the streets tonight In an everlasting kiss (metaphor for the heaven of being with you)

The highway's jammed with broken heroes on a last chance power drive

(giving it all they have in one last desperate hope)
Everybody's out on the run tonight but theres no place left to hide (feeling closed in)
Together Wendy we'll live with the sadness I'll love you with all the madness in my soul (All I am and have got will be yours...)
Someday girl I don't know when were gonna get to that place (We'll always have hope, no matter how dim)
Where we really want to go and well walk in the sun (Even if it's only a dream...)
But till then tramps like us baby we were born to run (hope in the midst of a hard life. Acknowledging the reality, but fighting it)

Like many of the songs on the album of the same name, there is a flower of hope in the writing of Springsteen. Yeah, life can be difficult, life can be hard and there may appear to be no way out of the life we're in now. But, if we just keep hoping, keep on moving, there's something better up ahead. This is the Voice of Springsteen. Looking at life, and putting it into words.

Of course, your view on the lyrics might be different than mine. That's okay. It's just some ideas.

Sunshine in a bottle (2008-06-12 16:20)

Sunshine, infused with irony
Like, joy from a bottle
3 refills by years end
Relief is fleeting, only
Lasts until the next round of
Sunshine in a bottle

The child proof cap is
no deterrent from
The apparent ease of instant
Salvation from a bottle

Ok, now I'm really pissed! (2008-06-13 08:28)

I've long known that the so called "news" network FoX "News" (We report, you decide *snort*) was a tool of the Right Wing, peopled by tools, and watched by tools. Anyone with half a farking brain knows that Fox "News" wouldn't know the truth if it bit them in the ass. Now, there's this latest tidbit of bullshit from Fox ~~Lies~~ News Network.

It appears that they had a graphic calling Michelle Obama his "baby momma." Hardly the stuff of credible, responsible journalists. Not that anyone with a modicum of sense, or the ability to think would ever confuse those dolts with real journalists. This borders on racism of the highest degree, and coupled with other recent ill-conceived or outright stupid/racist/misleading comments from FoX "News" whacko's, it shows a trend. To use fear, racism, lies and character assassination to help defeat Obama in the fall.

The scary thing is, in this day and age of the Cult of Stupid, there are people who accept as Gospel whatever comes out of the mouths of FoX "News" employees. They don't question, they don't read, they don't THINK. And there are nuts that are believed on other networks as well. I despise Lou Dobbs with a passion that borders on a disease. That man is a racist. Period. His border security focus is solely on the Mexican border, he also wouldn't know the truth if it bit him in the ass, has been confronted with his errors of fact and attacks those who dare to correct him. Hate must be good T.V. It sure ain't Journalism.

Absence makes the heart... (2008-06-18 10:12)

I went to the well
But the well was dry
Nary a drop of inspiration
Not even a mote of dust
A plethora of absence
Mixed with a sea of zilch...

I got nothin'

sigh

The Cynic Is Awake (2008-06-30 14:08)

You are a Cynic
Nothing is ever what it seems
Hidden meanings and motives
A fearsome cabal of conspiracies
Lurk behind every wall

Foolish youth, you have
Lost before you have begun
You can't believe in anything
So you choose to believe in Nothing...

The Cynic appears cool, detached.
So very wise, knowing of the ways.
It is a mask to hide behind
Keeping at bay disappointment
Or not even bothering to try

Cynicism is laziness
No need to get involved
Nothing is ever as it seems
Including, it would appear,
              Your pose...

_____-

Eh...it seems that something is missing from this. I'm not sure what. I need some nits picked, so please....jump right in.

Writer's Block: Home is... (2008-07-01 10:39)

LJ Question: Where do you call home?

Home, Home on the Range...

Or maybe not.

Home is where my heart is, which means it is wherever I am with my wife. Sounds sappy, but it is true. Our home is little more than bricks, wallboard, copper pipes and wiring. That's not a home, but a home is someplace to feel safe, warm, secure. And wherever she is, that's how she makes me feel. So, home is with her.

A Cynical Pose (2008-07-01 12:17)

Ok, here's the rewrite...

actually, it's probably the 4th version...I never rewrite that much.

I guess I feel like I'm onto something here...

The Cynical Pose

Before you, A Cynic
Nothing is ever what it seems
       (*LIES, LIES, NOTHING BUT LIES*)
A fearsome cabal of intrigue
Lurks behind every wall

Foolish youth, you have
Lost before you have begun.
       (*WITH SO MUCH BEFORE YOU*)
Since you're faith in "everything"
Has been found wanting
(*LIES, LIES, NOTHING BUT LIES*)
   You choose to believe in nothing
       nothing at all...

Wrapped up in your cloak or Urbanity,
Secure in your detachment,
   your chic sense of cool disdain
A mask you choose to wear
       (*LIES, LIES, NOTHING BUT LIES*)
Keeping disappointment at bay
Holding yourself in, trembling...

You think, you believe
That you are the only one
To have been deceived, played the fool
Have your belief in others shattered
       (*LIES, LIES, NOTHING BUT LIES*)
   You are not unique in this
      Nor are you alone...

Before you, The Cynic
Lazy is this approach
No thought required

Choices already made, no need to grow
        Position taken
Life as a holding pattern
Nothing is ever as it seems
  Including, it appears,
      your pose
          (lies, lies, nothing but lies...)

Writer's Block: Getting Closer Than Perhaps Expected
(2008-07-03 13:10)

LJ Question: Have you ever crushed on your closest friend?
Did you keep it secret, were there problems or did it blossom into something more?

LOL! No. My closest friends have always been guys. Until I met my wife, that is. I'm just not wired to crush on guys, so it was never an issue.

Book Review: Ranger's Revenge by James J. Griffin (2008-07-07 14:21)

Ranger Jim Blawcyzk returns in this, Griffin's 7th novel. Griffin has grown rapidly as a writer, proving that you get better by doing and not wishing.

The basic plot has renegades ambushing Blawcyzk when he at home, attacking his wife and son and leaving them all for dead, while rustling off their stock in the process. This puts Ranger Blawcyzk in a killing rage, as he disobeys orders to track down the ranny's who attacked his family.

There was a higher level of violence in this particular book, and quite a few lead belly aches administered by either Blawcyzk or his associates. The anger and barely controlled rage dissipates through the book, but not in a fashion I can truly believe in. Rather than that expected mental tussle with his faith in God, or with his calling as a lawman, Blawcyzk just sort of winds down and wants to bring them in, rather than gun them down. No real reason beyond physical fatigue is given. For me, that was a bit of a letdown, as the chance to witness a serious mental struggle was lost.

Blawcyzk is an atypical series character in the Western Genre and Griffin has done a wonderful job in fleshing out the character over the course of 6 books (one was about another character). He has given us insights into what makes Blawcyzk tick and the kind of man he really is. That's why the lack of serious attention to the struggle internally is bothersome to me.

Still, for all that, Griffin writes a good adventure yarn, with plenty of page turning action. If you like lots of riding and shooting in your westerns (which I do) then you'll enjoy this book. Available from the Silverjack Publishing web site or from Jim's own web site (tell 'im Mark sent ya....) The autographed copies don't cost anymore than the regular copies...so what are you waiting for?!?

What, exactly is Freedom of Speech? (2008-07-07 22:16)

"If we don't believe in free expression for people we despise, we don't believe in it at all." -Noam Chomsky

Who also said...

"If you believe in freedom of speech, you believe in freedom of speech for views you don't like. Goebbels was in favor of freedom of speech for views he liked. So was Stalin. If you're in favor of freedom of speech, that means you're in favor of freedom of speech precisely for views you despise."

Are these ideals you agree with or not?

I tire of people complaining about being offended. I don't know where it says in the U.S. Constitution that there is a Right to Not Be Offended...

The collection has run amok... (2008-07-09 20:50)

At what point does a collection become an accumulation? When the purpose isn't so much to be complete but to simply have?

I think that bridge was crossed some time ago in my life. I now have over 30 long boxes of comics in my home. Plus, there are at least 5-6 long boxes of trade paperbacks, hardbacks and Archive Editions/Marvel Masterworks type books. It has gotten out of hand. It's like Lex Luthor has take over my comic collecting mind and made me lose the notion of focus...AUGH!

I almost dread going to the comic shop on Wednesday's because I don't quite enjoy the comics as much as I used to. They aren't as fun to read as they used to be for me. What other people think of them is irrelevant to me. I am buying comics with characters in them that aren't fun to read. I buy them out of some misguided sense of loyalty, or hope they will get better.

Feh!

Enough of this, I say. When the current Phantom story ends (gotta see how it ends, don't ya know...) I drop it. Zorro gets the axe as well, and sadly so does the Angel and Buffy books. Whedon may be involved, but they aren't nearly as good as the TV shows were, and they are as confusing as hell, to be honest. There are some other books that will be dropped as well. I may just bail on all the Batman books as well. The idea of bringing Bruce back to what he was like before the Crisis is a good one. Sadly, DC Editorial can't seem to decide what Bat they want. It's all so frustrating. In fact, Final Crisis may just be my DC swan song.

Except for the Legion of Super-Heroes. A book I never cared much about, I've managed to pull together almost a complete collection from the early 70's until now without a tremendous outlay of cold, hard, rock 'n roll cash. Which is a good thing. (well, except for the Treasury edition with the wedding of Saturn Girl and Lightning Lad that I dropped a chunk for...in stellar condition)

So, what is the point of all of this? Mainly that I will be unloading boxes of comics in the coming months. eBay may well become my friend. There will be lots of old Spider-Man stuff going away. Lots and lots of Trade paperbacks at great prices...and I'll benefit with the increase in space and lightening of my load. The money will be nice, but it's not really the main reason for doing this. It's mainly to make this stuff go away and go to places that will appreciate it.

Writer's Block: In the Shoes of an Extravagant Restaurant Owner (2008-07-10)

LJ Question: If you started a restaurant, what would it serve, what would it look like and what would you name it? You have an unlimited budget.

This question, for some reason, makes me think of the classic song by Brownsville Station called The Martian Boogie. The phrase, "Fine scarfin' establishment like 'EAT'" has stuck with me for years. I also enjoy classic comfort food such as that found at the typical diner.

So, I'd have a bizarre looking building, call it EAT and serve diner food. And Falafels. Just because I really, really like them. We'd also have a little guy painted green hanging around the place during the overnight hours. Just to give the place some character and ambiance...

Movie Review: Batman: Gotham Knight (2008-07-14 11:23)

With the new Batman movie set to debut this weekend, we are in store for another round of Bat-mania, which is only right, I suppose.

DC Direct releases this direct to video Batman film to allow us a glimpse to what happens to him in his early days. There are a series of 6 vignettes, each by different art teams, with different character designs and different approaches to Batman.

It's done in a gritty Anime style, and while I like a lot of anime, it's not the best way to sell Batman to kids. I realize that anime is huge with kids today, and that's great. However, you probably won't win many converts to your character just by dressing him up in anime clothes if the stories stink. Solid stories cover up a multitude of sins and this one isn't the best in that department.

For example, the first story ("Have I Got a Story For You") is a riff on a 30 year old Batman story where kids all talk about how they have seen Batman and how each kid sees him differently. Except for the kid who was waiting on his buds to show at the skate park. He didn't see Batman until he came crashing through to window, looking nothing like his friends descriptions. The animated series did a better job of telling this story, so why it was done again is a mystery.

The story "Crossfire" didn't focus on Batman, but he was the 500 lb. gorilla in the corner just the same. It was a solid story, but again, it's been told before.

Outside of the extreme violence, there wasn't much original here. Nothing groundbreaking as the original Animated Series, or nothing that makes this must see Batman cartoons. Which is a shame.

Actually, the one bit that was worth seeing is the preview piece for the Wonder Woman animated movie to be released next spring. That looked loads better than this tired Batman movie.

Writer's Block: Food Loves and Hates (2008-07-14 11:51)

LJ Question: What foods can you not live without, and what foods can you not stomach?

I read several answers and I was surprised by the number of cheesy people and the lack of that staple of pantries everywhere, and the absolute hands down, Food of the Gawds, PEANUT BUTTER!!!!

I mean, has anyone ever written a song about cheese? No! They haven't! What does that tell you?

Peanut butter has a song written about it, and I present the lyrics here for your enjoyment, edification and to create cravings for the most wondrous of foods, Peanut Butter!

(I first heard this song as recorded by the J. Geils Band. If you don't know who they are, shame on you!)

Peanut Butter -J. Geils Band

There's a food goin' around
That's a sticky, sticky, goo
(Peanut, peanut butter)
A-well, it tastes real good
But it's so hard to chew
(Peanut, peanut butter)

All my friends tell me
That they dig it the mo-ho-ost
(Peanut, peanut butter)
Early in the morning
When they spread it on to-oh-oast
(Peanut, peanut butter)

I like peanut butter
Creamy, peanut butter,
Chunky, peanut butter, too

'Come on now, take a lesson, now!'
(Peanut, peanut butter)
'Open up your jaw, now!'
(Peanut, peanut butter)
'Spread it on your cracker, now!'
(Peanut, peanut butter) '

Stop, now' (Peanut, peanut butter)

I like peanut butter
Creamy, peanut butter,
Chunky, peanut butter, too

We-eee-ell I went to a dinner
And-a what did they e-e-eat?
(Peanut, peanut butter)
A-well, I took a big bite
And it stuck to my te-e-eeth
(Peanut, peanut butter)

Now, ev'rybody looks
A-like they've got the mumps
(He loves peanut butter)
Eat his peanut butter
In-a great big hunk
(He loves peanut butter)

I like peanut butter
Creamy, peanut butter
Chunky, peanut butter, too

I like peanut butter
Creamy, peanut butter
Chunky, peanut butter, too.

Writer's Block: Favorite Lyrics (2008-07-15 09:17)

LJ Question: What song lyrics would you love to have written, and why?

I love music. It's such a part of who I am, and how I allow myself to get in touch with my feelings. I've loved a lot of songs over the years, and as a (sort of) writer, I've admired the lyrics of others.

This song, while dealing with romantic love, can also be viewed as platonic or familial love. You may or may not know that I am estranged from my daughter. It haunts me on a daily basis. I wish I'd written this song because it is so clear, so perfectly states the emptiness inside that I feel from her not being a part of my life and my being a part of her life. Love is something you do, it's an action. Or it should be, at any rate. A choice you make on a daily basis. Every time I head this, I think of that little girl, grown now, and I fight a tear. Sometimes, I give in...

Gary Moore *Still Got The Blues*

Used to be so easy to give my heart away
But I found out the hard way
There's a price you have to pay
I found out that love was no friend of mine
I should have known time after time

So long, it was so long ago
But I've still got the blues for you

Used to be so easy to fall in love again
But I found out the hard way
It's a road that leads to pain
I found that love was more than just a game
You're playin' to win
But you lose just the same

So long, it was so long ago
But I've still got the blues for you

So many years since I've seen your face
Here in my heart, there's an empty space
Where you used to be

So long, it was so long ago
But I've still got the blues for you

Though the days come and go
There is one thing I know
I've still got the blues for you.

Book Review: <u>Hard Driving -The Wendell Scott Story</u> by Brian Donovan (2008-07-16 08:31)

I'm not a huge NASCAR fan. I feel compelled to state that up front. I've watched some over the years, and when it was more of a regional sport and the cars looked more like something you could actually buy, it was more fun for me. As NASCAR has increased in popularity, it has decreased in interest for me, personally.

After reading Donovan's biography of Wendell Scott, I was left with the same set of feelings I had when I visited the Negro League Museum in Kansas City. First, an appreciation for the stories of what Men of Passion were willing to do to chase their dreams and do the things they loved. The stories of Men and the inspiration that could be had from their stories of overcoming overwhelming odds.

Secondly, I feel shame. Shame that other white people could, would and did some of the awful things to another person simply because of their color. Wendell Scott never set out to be a trailblazer or make a racial statement. Wendell Scott wanted to drive race cars for a living. That he chose to do this in the Red Neck world of NASCAR, in the Deep South with Jim Crow in full flower is a testament to his desire to do what he wanted to do.

Donovan does a fine job of showing the trials and tribulations that Scott faced, the overt racism both in and out of NASCAR, and the good and less than good people that helped or hindered Scott as he chased his dream. He also shows a side of NASCAR, both past and present to some degree, that they would rather not have aired. Namely that NASCAR was racist, that promises made to Scott by founder Bill France weren't honored, that NASCAR did nothing to ensure that Scott was treated fairly. He won a race in Jacksonville, and to avoid him getting a peck from the track Beauty Queen (naturally a white woman), they jobbed him out of the victory celebration at the time. It was later awarded to him, with no fanfare, and blown off to a scoring error. A fiction NASCAR still stands behind.

Wendell Scott was hardly perfect, but who of us is? He was the first of four (4!) Black Drivers to have driven in NASCAR races, and while never a huge winner, he was a competitive driver for quite some time. Donovan presents not only the story of Wendell Scott, but the story of NASCAR, Civil Rights struggles, political skullduggery and institutional racism. He addresses the fictions of the "Greased Lightning" movie starring Richard Pryor and Scott's lack of concern for accuracy. He paints a solid picture of a man trying to do something he loved, and how he overcame and dealt with obstacles. A highly recommended biography and history book.

A complimentary copy of this book was provided by the publisher for the purpose of this review as part of the LibraryThing Early Readers Program.

Music Review: INXS -Shabooh Shoobah (2008-07-17 10:11)

First off, this album should get serious demerits for the goofy album cover and album name. I mean, who can take anyone seriously who names and album Shabooh Shoobah? And what is that on the cover?

Once you listen to the first strains of "The One Thing" you're thinking, "who care?" You're wanting to hit the dance floor, boogie in your seat or dance in your bedroom. The sinuous bass, drum beat, keyboards and the pouty singing of the late Michael Hutchence grab ahold and don't want to let go. It segue's into "To Look At You" and you're off into early 80's dance/pop heaven.

Other gems include the pretty "Jan's Song", the funky "Spy of Love" and the anthematic closer "Don't Change." This last song is one of the best closing songs on an album ever, in my humble opinion.

I first was exposed to INXS during the fledgling days of MTV, back when MTV mattered and played music video's. I had this on cassette and listening to it now is like hearing from an old friend, whilst bringing back memories of driving through the country with this blasting out of an overtaxed cassette deck. I never warmed up to later INXS efforts as much as I did this one. It has remained an old and treasured friend.

Movie Review: The Dark Knight (2008-07-21 08:46)

This film is outstanding. So much so, that I will go see it again. I'm already waiting for the DVD release.

Heath Ledger was outstanding. He played The Joker the way I couldn't imagine anybody playing him and getting away with it. He wasn't an insane clown (with or without a posse), or the Crown Prince of Crime...no, Ledger pegged him as an instrument of Chaos, pure and simple. He went through life with the "Death Race 2000" rules in place...there ain't no rules.

This Joker strikes me as Definitive. At least on screen. Taking everything away from Romero and Nicholson, this performance blew us away. My wife said he played such a compelling creep (and creep is her harshest description for somebody...Cheney is creepy in her view), that while she wanted to look away, couldn't. She was mesmerized by this movie. And Aaron Eckhart portrayed Harvey Dent to perfection. His story is the main structure the movie is hung from and told. He is truly central to the plot, and the path of the movie. No spoilers in saying that it's tragic. It's been said that the Harvey/Two Face segment towards the end could have made a terrific third film, thus making the movie too long. If you agree with that, then you missed the point of Two Face in the movie. Every point that the movie (ham handedly) made was based on what happened to Harvey. Taking that part out of the film would have left it feeling quite incomplete.

Bale was fine, not great, but better than anyone in the Burton fiasco's. Michael Caine was stellar and the added importance of Morgan Freeman's Lucius Fox allows him to shine. Pacing was good, even for a film this long. I only looked at my watch once, and that was at the end. It's a terrific movie, and easily one of my favorite comic-to-film adaptations.

Writer's Block: Cramming Yourself into a Sentence (2008-07-21 09:32)

LJ Question: Try to describe yourself in one sentence.

I am an amazingly wonderful human being!

Yeah, I think that pretty well covers it. Except for the mistakes I've made. Some of which continue to bite me in the ass. Some of which I'd like to make amends, but am not able to or allowed to.

What I am, is forgiven by G*d for being the miserable sinner that I am.

Baseball Boy meets Dr. Botany (and The Sprout) (2008-07-21 09:38)

Ok, so I can actually hear the "WTF"s" going on in assorted people's minds. Good. Keeps you on your toes....

I belong to many Yahoo Groups. Have for years. One that I am particularly fond of and enjoy the most is KirbyKomics. It's mainly a bunch of guys my age (give or take) who share many similar interests. Comics, cars, food, family, bad jokes, pop culture, literature and "spirited discussion" about topics like Religion and such. They really are one of the finest collections of men I've ever run across and I count myself fortunate to count these guys amongst my friends.

As you might expect, there's a lot of give and take on this list. As in, giving and taking loads of sh!t. Putdowns, insults, and general guy stuff. Saying things to each other we'd never say were our wives around, or any other Lady present. Mean, nasty things like Dr. Tom Lammers ending up with the nickname Dr. Botany! Protector of Plants and what have you (it's a bunch of old comic geeks! What on earth did you expect?!?) And since I love the game of baseball,
I got stuck with the nickname (mean, I tell ya...) of Baseball Boy (I'm actually one of the younger members of this group).

Tom and his Undergraduate Assistant, Laura (code named The Sprout) are working at the Botanical Gardens in St. Louis, working on some hyper secret project that I'm sure will have dire consequences for Mankind As We Know It! Actually, he's working on verifying findings on a colleagues paper and he gets to hang out in St. Louis for a month. During the hottest time of the year, to boot! He leads such a charmed life...

So, I called him and challenged him to lunch at 20 paces. He accepted and we agreed to meet at a Steak 'n Shake in Wentzville, MO. I rode the Gold Wing in the blistering summer heat (felt like the inside of a blast furnace outside yesterday...heat index over 100) 80 miles one way. Tom walked in to the eatery, and after the customary and overly used battle between heroes due to confusion, we finally agreed to attack our common enemy: Lunch! (we won!) In person, Tom is exactly as he appears online. Nice, polite, witty, self-deprecating and genuine. I am glad we had the chance to meet in person. His assistant Laura was a nice young lady and enjoys the work that they are doing. What was refreshing was that her eyes didn't glaze over and roll back into her head as us Olde Guys talked Olde Guy stuff.

After a nice visit of about an hour and a half, we took pictures to immortalize such an auspicious occasion and agreed to do something similar again when he returns to Missouri in January. So, astride my trusty Gold Wing (wishing it had A/C) I returned home to my lovely wife. We went out to dinner at the HuHot and enjoyed a wonderful dinner.

So, there ya have it. The first Titanic Meeting between Dr. Botany (And The Sprout) & Baseball Boy (who needs a more adult name...)

A couple of photo's from the historic and epic meeting!

<u>Mark and Tom</u>

The Botanical Duo! The Sprout (Laura) and Dr. Botany! (Tom)

Accumulation Reduction... (2008-07-22 09:57)

Well, the beginning phases of the soon to be legendary Comic Reduction of Accumulation Project (C.R.A.P.) has begun! I unloaded some 300 comics recently in a deal that netted me some nice cash plus the equally valuable benefit of more space. Of course, there are so many comics yet, that it is hard to tell. However, Rome not having been built (or even falling) in a day, I figure a good first step is worth noting.

In fact, it was the bulk of a group of comics I figured I'd have to give away. They were all a part of the Clone Saga from the Spider-Man books of over a decade ago. So, I got good coin, the purchaser got good value and I also got some more room....

Use of a Writing Prompt (2008-07-23 09:41)

On the all _unwritten group, moderator lady _aduial posted the following prompt:

"love at first sight"

This was what I wrote from those four words;

"Love at first sight...is often cured by a second glance." Words my Grandmother lived by. Not just with people, but in life. She went on to say, "Looks can be deceiving, so search for the truth of things before getting all whopperjawed over something or somebody..." Grandma was a smart lady.

On Recent Quietude (2008-07-30 11:21)

My wife and I went to the City so nice, they named it twice for a week of Big Apple living.

Too many things to tell in one post, so I'll parse them out over the next few days.

It's nice to be home, but I'm tired as all get out. So is my other half. We had a great time, however.

On New York (Part, The First) (2008-07-31 14:00)

Rain. Last Thursday, as it has so many days this year, it rained. Loading a car for vacation in the rain is a new experience for me. Now that I've done it, I don't care to do it again. I'm not one much for seeing omens in things, so the rain was a mere annoyance. However, coupled with the slow service at the bank, it could have been seen as a warning of sorts. The poor schlub at the bank, I sort of felt sorry for him. He didn't know how to do things like load a gift card, and when he found the procedure instructions, they'd been changed again. If I hadn't been in a hurry, it would have been amusing.

With the rain, and the delay at the bank, we were in danger of being late to the airport. That's a 2 hour drive (at least) from our place, and Kansas City International Airport is out in the middle of nowhere. And I never quite remember how to get there, so that added to the stress level. Upon arrival, leaving the car in long term parking and getting checked in, we found out that the plane was delayed about an hour so the rushing around was all for naught. To make matters scarier, we misheard an announcement that "our" flight was delayed for another 2 hours. Turned out to be a false alarm, which was refreshing. Before this turns into a step by slogging step account of our recent trip, I only mention these events to illustrate how things can start out in less than stellar fashion and rapidly rise from there.

So, we did a lot of walking in New York. Our first night there, I ended up with a couple of blisters. Probably more a function of worn out socks (they ended up getting tossed) and shoes not being tight enough more than anything else. Still, it made walking the next day a little trickier. We stayed in an older hotel that had pretty small rooms, nice sized private bath, that was located right off 5th Avenue. We were 6 blocks from the Empire State Building in one direction and just a few blocks from the Flatiron Building in the other. Nicely located for most everything we wanted to do.

Rather than go over each one individually today, I'll just leave you with some of my impressions of the city. Such as the mix of smells. They ranged from aftershave to exhaust, to perfume trails and sex, food from vendors and garbage piled on the sidewalk waiting for collection. The smells of culture were everywhere, and you could experience them just be walking. It was interesting to me to watch people congregating on the sidewalk, outside of a small pub or club, drinks in hand, with piles of trash nearby studiously being ignored and accepted as part of the landscape. The things you get used to, I suppose.

I've got to say that New Yorkers get a bad rap. Seriously. By and large, everyone we met from the city was unfailingly polite, very helpful and downright nice. We needed help on the subway? We got it. We needed directions somewhere? Not a problem. Even the fans at both NY ballparks were pleasant to talk to and joke with. The cranky, jaded, cynical New Yorker would probably be known as the town crank in a smaller town, patted on his head and sent on his way. People are people pretty much wherever you go, in my experience.

Lombardi's for pizza; ESPNZone for sports food and a terrific waitress; the Lexington Candy Shop Luncheonette for awful service and an egg cream; Big Daddy's Diner for expensive diner food and wonderful service (free refills!); Halal Food from a street vendor who taught me how to say "Hurry" in Arabic, which I promptly forgot within 3 blocks; hot dogs in Central Park; Brooklyn Bagel Cafe on 5th Avenue for breakfast twice; and on and on.

Walking across the Brooklyn Bridge; The Metropolitan Museum of Art; Central Park; a boat ride in the East River to see the Waterfalls of New York City; The Empire State Building, Yankees Stadium; Times Square; Shea Stadium; walking up Park Avenue; St. Patrick's Cathedral and so many other things that we saw and did. An amazing trip for a couple of Mid-Westerners. It was easy for me to see why people love New York. There was a sense of life and vitality that I've not felt elsewhere (sorry Chicago) and there really is always something to do. That's why I am so bone tired. We tried to do as many of those things as we could in a short time. We can't wait to go back. The best part was being with my wife, pretty much alone for the entire time. It was a great vacation for the two of us.

Fearing the Monkey! (2008-07-31 14:17)

A friend and I were chuckling over a recent Get Fuzzy strip where the phrase "Fear the Monkey" was used. He commented that he thought it would make a great battle cry...with that in mind, I offered this in return;

"And the hordes of Elves, Goblins and Trolls spilled down the Mountain of Ish, the fierce battle cry, "FEAR THE MONKEY" ringing from the many hills...."

Which got me to thinking....(RUN! FLEE! WHILE YOU CAN!!! SAVE YOURSELF!)

——— And it came to pass, during the Days of the Ascension of The Monkey, that a prophecy was handed down. From the Prophets of the Mountains of Ishtar came the following:

> And from the East shall He come. He shall come, full of power, full of wisdom and full of glory (and not a little of himself) to smite down the Monkey. After the Days of the Ascension of the Monkey shall come the Darkening Days, yea, the Nights of the Descent of The Monkey shall come and they shall be terrible. Full of dread, fear, trembling and much hysteria (and endless reruns of Leave it to Beaver) shall accompany the Nights of the Descent of the Monkey. It shall be as a teenage boy with a new car, it shall last 1,000 years or longer (maybe less. Who can say with prophecies?). Nobody will recognize The Savior of the Monkey, nor will they believe him to be who he says he is, as he will not be the first to claim to be who he says he is, just the first to actually BE who he says he is. May the Gods preserve the Monkey. May the Gods save us all.

Many wept after that prophecy was handed down, for none knew exactly what it meant. Including the Prophets.

Fear the Monkey, indeed...

More Monkey Business (2008-08-01 14:45)

Today's prompt, combined with a lack of serious rest for my weary bones, and the continued raging of serious Monkey Fear...brings me to this unholy place....

The prompt, from all unwritten is: lace and corsets (Now would be a good time to RUN!!!)

> Many have wondered about the Power of the Monkey. From whence does the Monkey derive his awesomeness, is his very being suffused with power? Does he have a divine connection to the Gods from On High? Was he just born thattaway?
>
> Nay, seeker of truth and wisdom. The Monkey of the Power is derived from his raiment. His very clothing provide him with the channel to focus the dread Power of the Monkey. And the source, the locus of said dread power is the lace and corsets that decorate and pack His Immenseness into his Regal Monkey Suit of Armor.

Fear the Monkey, indeed...

Writer's Block: Loved Ones Afar (2008-08-04 11:09)

LJ Question: Do you miss anyone right now?
What past experiences with this person, or these persons, make it easy for you to miss them?

Do I miss someone? I miss several someones. This is one of those sucker questions. As in, I'm a sucker for these sort of questions...

I miss those who have gone to their reward. I thought of my mother quite a lot during our recent trip to NYC. She loved that city. I knew she'd been to St. Patrick's Cathedral and I had myriad thoughts of her whilst we were there.

I miss my Grandfathers. Granddad, I think I'm finally old enough to relate better to him and appreciate him even more than when I was younger. A great example of getting smart too late in life. Grandpa was just a good man and I miss him. Even more than 20 years later...

I miss some of the people I knew growing up. Some are alive and just missing and some aren't and will always be missing to me.

I miss my daughter. I was reminded of how when she was little she would walk up to women out in public and tell them, "I like your shoes." It always made me chuckle a little when she'd do that. It was just so darn cute. She was adorable when she was a little girl. Poor kid, when she was visiting me, I had no clue how to do her hair. She ended up looking like an unmade bed. She wanted to wear dresses, so I'd find her a dress and get all that taken care of. Then came time to fix her hair. What a disaster that was. I always felt so incompetent at times like that. Her mother always sent this well groomed, adorable little girl and I always returned a messy headed kid. She was clean, so were her clothes but it was apparent that Daddy hadn't a clue how to fix little girls hair. I miss that. I miss her climbing into my lap and telling me in that sweet voice daughters have as little people, "Daddy...I love you" and then she'd either hug me or drift off to sleep.

I miss my wife. I know I saw her this morning and that (G*d willing) I'll see her this evening. I just miss her when she's not there. She's such a part of me that when she isn't there, I realize it.

Writer's Block: Your ePet (2008-08-05 08:27)

LJ Question: What creature would your ideal electronic pet resemble? Would it resemble any? What would it look like?

Ok, this is absurdism in the extreme. WTF is an electronic pet? One of those stupid things you use as a key chain? Is it for people who can't hack having REAL pets?

What sort of clueless brain comes up with stupid crap like this? Fer the love of G*WD! Spare me from mindless drivel such as this!

Puh-Leeze!

And just to play along, if I were gonna have me a fake pet, it'd resemble a wolverine. Trained to attack stupid people, rend them limb from limb, and gorge on their innards, feast on the eyeballs and brains...with veins hanging from their electronic teeth. Taking plenty of digital photographs complete with Photoshop'd circles and arrows and a paragraph embedded in the file description... Virtually, of course. Can't have the streets awash in the blood of idiots, can we? ;-)

Review: Georgie James -Places (2008-08-06 08:31)

In looking at the Top 20 on my Last.fm charts, I realize that I am no longer hip and musically happenin'. Fact of life. I'm outside the "Cool" 18-34 demographic and have been for nigh on a decade. Fact of life. Of the 20 artists in my personal Top 20, only 2 (Nicole Atkins & The Sounds) have started their careers in the last 10 years.

Fact of life. I stumbled across Georgie James whilst blog surfing a while ago. I listened to the album and liked it, but didn't visit it again for a while. When I did, I was totally blown away (Totally, dude...gotta keep it Olde Skool). These two from Washington, D.C. had something special going on this, their debut album.

Georgie James consists of John Davis & Laura Burhenn. Davis was the drummer of Q and Not U and Burhenn had released several solo recordings before forming Georgie James. They went with their mutual strengths and love of similar 60's and 70's era pop and rock. That's the sonic pallet they mine and use to good effect, while taking on current thoughts and concerns in their lyrics. The harmonies are sharp and tight, and the trading off of lead vocals between Davis and Burhenn works quite well and is effective.

Stand out tracks include the first single "Need Your Needs" which chugs along in a marvelous power pop vein, and "Cake Parade" is another stellar song on this, their only album. I say that because I read on their web site earlier this week that this will be the only Georgie James release as they've called it a day and disbanded. A shame, that. This was a group that could have grown and created wonderful music for many years. The evidence is on "Places"

I had one of these... (2008-08-07 07:06)

I toted mine around while I delivered my newspapers on my paper route. I think I had about four 8 tracks at the time. It was handy for that because I didn't have to set it down to change the track it was playing. I just sort of held it out and snapped my wrist, sort of like a flick or something and the handle stayed put, but the player moved, activating the switch. I was so damn cool, lemme tell ya... I still think of this silly player when I listen to The Rolling Stones "Goats Head Soup" album.

Writer's Block: Less Than Idle Hands (2008-08-07 08:11)

LJ Question: Do you have any odd nervous habits?

Aside from the usual run of the mill tics and odd mannerisms that make people unique (putting car keys in my ear to scratch those damnable itches), I have a few pretty standard knee jerk reactions.

- I wanna bitch slap people who are idiotic mouth breathers who think they know something. Especially when it is patently obvious they wouldn't know how to spell their own name without the help of the drivers license they carry around. What people are these? The freakin' idiots who never bother to read anything, get all their so-called information from the talking heads on TV and believe, honestly BELIEVE they know all they need to about something! Stupid people, and I mean willfully ignorant dolts...not the poor people who have problems and do the best they can...make me see a murderous haze. Reminds me of the bit in that old song,

> And I went up there, I said, "Shrink, I want to kill. I mean, I wanna, I wanna kill. Kill. I wanna, I wanna see, I wanna see blood and gore and guts and veins in my teeth. Eat dead burnt bodies. I mean kill, Kill, KILL, KILL." And I started jumpin up and down yelling, "KILL, KILL," and he started jumpin up and down with me and we was both jumping up and down yelling, "KILL, KILL." And the sargent came over, pinned a medal on me, sent me down the hall, said, "You're our boy."

- People who are willfully, with malice aforethought, cruel. There's enough nastiness in the world. Why the hell would you go out of the way to be an asshat? This creates in me the desire to tie the miscreant to the ground, pour honey all over her/him and let ants do their happy dance all over them. Only for an hour or three. Wouldn't want to be too big a jerk about it, right?

- People who are entirely too sensitive. Who look for reasons to be offended. As a result, they want people fired for saying something they don't like. For taking a position that is contrary to their world view. Fucktards, who believe in the First Amendment insofar as it applies to them, but not the other guy. Too many have died for that right. I wanna lock idiots like this up in a small room, flooded with lights, and make them listen to "Don't Worry, Be Happy" on repeat for a couple of days. That'll fix their Politically Correct asses.

I could go on, but you get the point. Stupid people who want to control others and bring them down to their level of ignorance royally piss me off. They induce in me all manner of automatic reactions.

I'll wrap this up on a more positive note. I cry when I see Old Glory and am reminded of those who served Our Country, died for Our Country to protect the ideals and beliefs that flag represents. The Star-Spangled Banner, at times, has brought me to tears. Because there is absolutely no way I can ever express my gratitude to those who served what the flag represents.

More Monkey Business, pt. 2 (2008-08-07 12:27)

After the Prophecy of The Monkey and pondering the The Power of the Monkey, there was much fear and trembling, not to mention more than a bit of loathing, and some gnashing of teeth thrown in for good measure. Nobody understands the awesome Power of the Monkey, least of all, The Monkey.

The Prophecy could be read in so many different ways, and confusion (more than usual) reigned across the Lands. So much so that war, rumors of war and a War reunion tour went forth. The battle cry, "FEAR THE MONKEY" was heard ringing from hill and dale, from stream to ocean and during reruns of "The Cosby Show." The inclination of most of the residents of the Lands, was to run away. Far, far away. Alas, the Power of the Monkey was such that, there was no running away from The Monkey.

Shame, that. Especially in light of what was to come...

On Brett Favre (2008-08-07 12:41)

I am so glad that the Brett Favre saga is going to be over soon. At least the constant media barrage part of it. I'll be glad to get back to over exposure of Obama and McCain with the occasional blip from Paris Hilton. Sportscenter will no longer be WALL-TO-WALL Brett Favre coverage. ESPNRadio will no longer have the Brett Favre Watch, with updates on when he wiffled and when he waffled. Life will soon return to a sense of normalcy. Red Sox Nation will be whining about how hard it is to be Red Sox fans, even though the Yankees aren't a contender this season (The Tampa Bay Rays? Who knew?). We will still be waiting for the Chicago Cubs to have their Annual June Swoon (doesn't matter what month it is, and this year it ain't gonna happen) and the LA Angels of Anaheim (Orange County, California, U.S.A., North America, Planet Earth, Solar System...you get the idea here) will quietly continue to be the best TEAM in MLB...

And yet, I'm sorry to see that Favre is going to be like Montana, and Simpson and Namath. All great players who stayed one or two seasons too long. Who ended their careers with a team they weren't synonymous with. I mean, Favre as a NY Jet? That's nuts! At least to this Packer fan, it is.

I gotta say, I loved watching Brett Favre play football. I remember when he wasn't the grizzled object of Man Crushes in Press Boxes nationwide, but just a kid who played hard, won hard and lost hard. That iconic moment when he threw that first TD Pass in Super Bowl 31? (no roman numbers for me...) Running off the field with his helmet in the air, for all the world like a kid screamin' to his dad, "Hey! Look what I Did!"

I'm gonna miss No. 4 under center, rolling, ducking, running around behind the line of scrimmage looking to make something, hell ANYTHING happen. Even if it's wrong. That's the thing about Favre. He did things nobody had ever seen before. He wasn't afraid of failure. He was afraid of not trying. Of not going for it. It would either be chicken salad or chicken shit, but it would be something. In some respects, it was almost fitting that his last play as a Packer was an interception. He has two records that are significant. Most TD's and Most Pick's for a career. Favre tried and came up short in the NFC Championship Game.

Favre really was an everyman. I don't fault him for his inability to decide to walk away from something he so clearly loves. The demands are harder on a 38 year old football player than it was when he was a kid. He's been through so much, and we were along for the ride. Favre really is a what you see is what you get kind of guy. There isn't any dissembling with him. He really is conflicted. He really didn't want to be a distraction for his former teammates. He really doesn't know from one day to the next whether he wants to play football or not. He also believes he was wronged by the

Packers, and his hurt feelings really got the better of him.

Favre wanted to do something. Even if it was wrong. This is in character with his whole career. It's who he is. It's what made him such a compelling football player. It doesn't get shut off when he walks off the field. This whole episode just goes to show you that Brett Favre is really Brett Favre.
I wish him well with The Jets, and thanks for all the memories. The good ones, the not so good ones, and for showing up every Sunday for 16 years.

If Only (Aug. 7th, 2008 at 2:54 PM)

IIf only
   Your view could be mine
   To see you as I do
   Would open your eyes

If only
   I could get inside
   To see you as you do
   The secrets that you keep

If only
   I could understand
   Why you miss what I see
   What makes you special

If only
   How the little things
   Your Pretty Smile
   A laugh, warm my heart

If only
   For five minutes
   What I see and feel
     About you could be
   What you see and feel
     About you

If only...

More on New York (2008-08-08 09:29)

The recent trip to New York brought some things to mind I'd never really thought about. In no particular order, these are some of notions that crossed not only my mind, but my wife's as well.

- Could easily give up driving. Mass Transit in NYC is amazing.
- Did we see the "real" New York" or just the touristy part? How to see the NYC that New Yorkers see?
- So much walking
- Egg Creams are no big deal.
- Onions in tomato sauce? On a hot dog? Don't knock it till you try it
- Everyone needs to try a knish. They are potato-ee love
- A Halal food vendor taught me to say "Hurry" in Arabic. I promptly forget it
- We were told not to look up, or we'd be branded as tourists. How could we not? So many beautiful buildings. I guess you get so accustomed to seeing them, they become commonplace.
- Too many buildings with scaffolding around them or in them.

The hurry scurry pace seemed to be less than I'd been lead to believe. It didn't seem as chaotic or as overwhelming as I would have expected. As I said earlier, I felt comfortable there in ways I never have here. Maybe it's the ability to disappear in a sea of people. To be above it all at the top of the Empire State Building and yet as inconsequential to those on the street as they are to people up there.

Going to Central Park was something wonderful. As many people as there were there, still the place exuded peace. We watched a bit of a league softball game on one of the diamonds. Very relaxing. Plenty of people just lolling in the grass, or the sun. Young ladies in bikini's sunbathing, with young men trying hard to look like they aren't looking. Right in the middle of one of the largest cities in the world.

The wall that separates people, that they put up in order to not become inundated with everything around them, comes down quickly when spoken to. We talked to all sorts of people on the subway. In fact, we were only blown off once in five days. I asked a guy in a security guard uniform if he could answer a question. He didn't stop walking as he said, "I don't know anything. It's how I stay alive" grinned like a jackal and kept on walking. We just laughed at his idiocy.

Once, we were lost in Brooklyn. Well, we knew where we were, but not how to get back to Manhattan other than walking back across the Brooklyn Bridge, or the Manhattan Bridge. We wanted a subway station is what we wanted. We'd already walked to Brooklyn and walking back didn't suit our tired legs, or blistered feet. So, I asked this guy whose job was to sit at the end of a driveway and watch people drive past which way to the subway. He spoke not one word of conversational English. Still, he recognized subway. So, he smiled (and he had a terrific smile), said "Subway" and pointed in the direction of a building on the other side of several others. I nodded, said "thanks" and we headed off in that general direction. We had little confidence that we would actually find anything, but by golly there was a seedy subway station. We went down into the bowels of Brooklyn, decided which train we needed to take and made it back to Manhattan. Actually, we ended up at Grand Central Station (where I took a picture of the sign to Track 29. If you have to ask, you are too young...) and eventually to where we wanted to go. Which, as I recall, was someplace to eat.

I've got scads of pictures. I took close to 500 photos. Digital Photography is a wonderful thing. This is the only photo I've actually uploaded anywhere.

I hope to upload some more in the coming days, just to show some of the interesting things we saw.

Saturday Ride (2008-08-11 20:41)

Saturday I got up at the unholy hour of 6 a.m. Unholy and unreasonable for Saturday, at any rate. I usually sleep in until 7:30 or so. Heaven help me, but I've turned into my dad. Getting sidetracked...

I met my friend Greg at one of the local Steak 'n Shake joints. Best kept secret for breakfast. I mean, an egg is an egg, right? So, the prices are great, not many people there so service is quite fast. Did I mention it's cheap? And at 7:00, there are usually more employees than customers. We filled up, paid up and headed out the door. It was 61 degrees at 7, and not much warmer at 8 when we finally got moving.

Greg had his new (to him) 1986 GL1200 Interstate Gold Wing (on the right) and my 1996 GL1500 Aspencade Gold Wing was ready to go. At the least, I had taken to time to clean the dead bugs off the windshield while Greg had cleaned everything off his bike. The shade doesn't allow you to see the shine on Greg's Interstate.

I own this motorcycle and a 2005 Suzuki Boulevard C50 Limited Edition (which means it's a lovely shade of Cop Attention Getting Red) and I'd love to sell that one and replace it with a recent vintage Royal Enfield Bullet 500 Classic in British Racing Green with the Pedestrian Slicer, solo seat and other nifty doo-dads and baubles. The onliest places in Missouri to even look at a Royal Enfield Bullet 500 would be someplace in Eldorado Springs and Interstate Motorcycles in Rolla. We chose Rolla.

Not to be outdone, we decided to make the ride more fun by adding more miles and not going the same way as we were coming home. We elected to take the wandering route in the morning and head straight for home in the afternoon. Turns out this was a good decision, mainly because we were more tired in the afternoon.

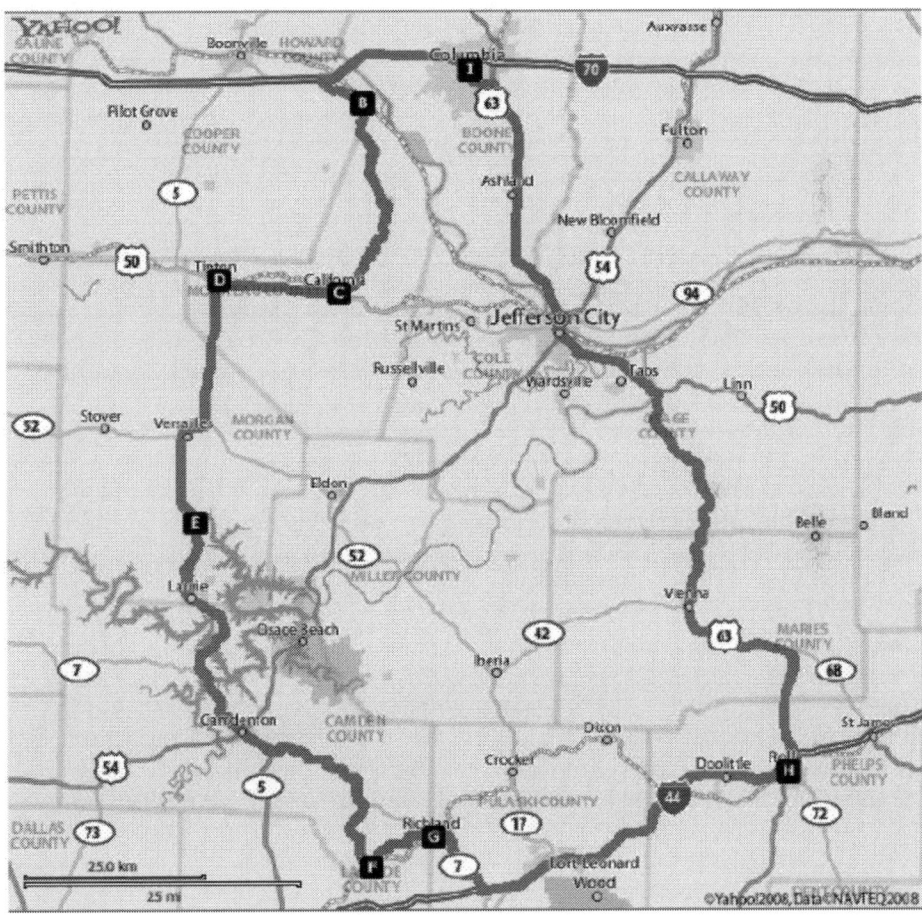

This is the route we ended up taking. Right around 300 miles. Which, when you stop to think about it, is a long way to go just to test ride a motorcycle you may not even want to buy. That was the excuse for the long ride so common sense wasn't really part of the equation. And just to makes things easy, we started in Columbia and went west on I-70 then South and west (again) and south then east to Rolla. As you can see, we went round Robin Hood's barn to get there. But the scenery was stunning in places.

Riding along St. Hwy 5 around Lake of the Ozarks was sort of like a trip down memory lane for me. I first got a motorcycle because the car I had at the time suffered catastrophic engine failure. The head gasket blew. By itself, it's not such a big deal. It's only a $25-40 part, plus a few other odds and ends. The bad news is, you have to take apart a huge chunk of the engine just to get there that by the time it's all said and done, on the conservative side, it's a $1500 repair. That car wasn't worth it. Believe it or not, the pastor of my church suggested the motorcycle as a viable alternative, so I found one that was cheaper than the repair bill and just let the car go. Easier that way...until winter came, but that's a whole nuther story.

I had to have transportation at the time as I had just taken a job at one of those concrete statuary places. If things worked out, I'd be the on site manager, have a place to live and pull a decent salary. Before I packed up and moved, I decided to play it safe and commute for a couple of weeks. Which meant I had to ride roughly 90 miles. Each way. I had to learn fast, lemme tell ya. The job didn't work out as the people who ran the business and I didn't get along too well. I was too formal for them, and he thought I was an idiot for buying a motorcycle to get to and from work rather than going in the toilet to buy another crappy car. I lasted a week before I quit. Good thing I didn't move. The good thing is I put close to 1,000 miles on the motorcycle in the first 2 weeks because I had no choice. I learned more about riding in that time than most folks do. Rode more, too.

So, whilst riding down memory lane and enjoying the scenery, we avoided cars. Because once we got near The Lake, traffic picked up along Hwy. 5. It's a great road for riding down, but I'd hate to be driving in a large car or something as the road is pretty narrow and not too straight. As a result, passing just isn't done. If you get stuck behind a poke, you're stuck until they turn or you get where your going. Since we weren't in a huge hurry, this was ok. However, driving past a pickup truck pulling a boat large enough to have its own zip code was a tad disconcerting. Actually, it provoked more of a, "Whatwazzat?" moment than anything else.

Leaving The Lake area behind us in Camdenton, we headed down towards Stoutland. That's the area where my beloved wife grew up and man is it beautiful. Rolling, quiet and not a little lonely in places. It was really odd hearing crickets singing loud enough to drown out the stereo on the Gold Wing in the middle of the day. We stopped at the school were my wife attended, and got a couple of odd looks from passersby as we stood there in the parking lot, me taking pictures. Ah well, the life of a tourist in Stoutland (Sa-Loot!)

We ambled on out of town and headed for I-44 and Rolla. I had never ridden or driven on this stretch of 44 before and the overpowering GREEN of all the trees almost overwhelmed my senses. It was stunning in its beauty and I'd love to go back in the fall. The color must be amazing as the vistas and views were outstanding. 30 miles of this and I was just enjoying the heck out of it. Remember, I-44 took the place of Historic and Beloved Route 66 and there's much to see.

Thundering along, we eventually made it to Rolla and Interstate Motorcycles. What a nice bunch of guys there. We talked a bit, mostly about bikes and such. After my legs were sufficiently stretched, I took a spin on a Royal Enfield Bullet 500 Deluxe. Totally different than riding the Gold Wing (weighs about 1/3 as much) and rides rougher. However, that's not a bad thing. Greg took a spin as well and both of us left favorably impressed. Both with the bike and the shop. That was a worthwhile trip.

We had some lunch, and then headed for home on Hwy. 63. I live within spitting distance of 63 and travel up and down it to Jefferson City fairly regularly. However, I'd never been south of Jeff City on 63 before so I had no idea what to expect. Which was more rolling, and beautiful country side. We were heading into the Gasconade River valley and there was a sign that said Scenic Look. On a whim, I pulled off. Greg opted not too because the road was gravel. His loss, I suppose. This is what I saw...

Can you imagine what that will look like in the Fall? And when I get a clue how to properly use the filters I have for my camera? I just stood there, gaping for a moment. The photo doesn't do it justice at all. A lot of clarity was lost when I took the picture. I hope it gives you an idea. I really was impressed with the view.

About an hour later, as we hit Columbia, we parted ways with a honk of our horns and a wave. Greg to his house and I to the store. My wife spent the day at home cleaning. I took her some flowers as a small token of my appreciation. She deserves that and so much more.

The capper to the day was dinner with some good friends from out of town who came through to see us. We enjoyed that. All in all, it was a terrific Saturday.

Except for the garage door crapping out. Oh well...

Writer's Block: Six-Word Story (2008-08-14 09:28)

LJ Question: Hemingway was once challenged to write a story in only six words. His response? "For sale: baby shoes, never worn." He is believed to have called it his greatest literary work ever. Can you write a story in six words?

He'd shot her. He was wrong.

You did what? With him? Really?

Writer's Block: The Meaning of Love (2008-08-25 15:03)

LJ Question: What does love mean to you, and why? Have you always felt this way?

Love means saying you're sorry, and meaning it, when you fuck up.

Love means "I am third"

John 15:13 "Greater love hath no man than this, that a man lay down his life for his friends."

This I Believe (2008-08-27 08:17)

No, it's not something I wrote...nor something I have thought about a whole lot, but it IS something I do.

I listen to "This I Believe" in podcast form via iTunes. Something I started fairly recently, to be honest. I believe that a person should never stop learning, and learning what others believe and how it affects their lives is more important than who was President Monroe's Vice President.

The following is something I've done my whole life. I've always spoken to people I don't know. Most of the time, they are friends I hadn't met yet. So, with that in mind, please take a couple of minutes and listen to Howard White explain "[1]The Power of Hello..." (Link takes you to the NPR site...)

1. http://www.npr.org/templates/story/story.php?storyId=93536198

Brave & The Bold 16 -Review (2008-08-28 16:42)

This particular series is so hit and miss these days, that I'm never quite sure what to expect. This issue had me chuckling at the cover, but that never means anything more in the DCU. Covers these days don't always give you a serious indication of what is going on inside. Sometimes, it's just Artists Wankarama making with pretty pictures that have nothing to do with the contents. But..I wander off topic!

Superman is often described as The Big Blue Boy Scout. Right or wrong, whatever it is that makes Big Blue the role model for other heroes, that's the perception. Teaming him up with Catwoman, who can be a hero or a thief, depending on what time it is or what her mood is, sounds like a recipe for disaster. However, that's not the case in this funny book.

Selina Kyle is an interesting character, and seldom moreso than in this issue. Most female characters in the DCU are too awestruck to react to Supes the way Kyle does. Pure, unadulterated, primal lust. She likes what she sees, and Clark being Clark, he doesn't know how to react to it. He doesn't trust her (with reason) and he has his hands full. The best bit is when they decide to crash an underworld auction in disguise. Catwoman dresses Superman up like Clark, who is damn near beside himself with panic as a result. Too funny.

In the end, Clark goes with his instincts. Not about Catwoman, but regarding Batman. Bruce trusts Selina and in the end, that's enough for Clark. If you want to read a comical comic book, this would be the issue to grab.

Writer's Block: What You'd Accomplish if Success Was Guaranteed
(2008-08-29 10:51)

LJ Question: Knowing beforehand that you wouldn't fail, what would you attempt to do?

I'd jump out of an airplane. Naked.

Writer's Block: Saving Money (2008-08-30 09:14)

LJ Question: What are some ways to save money on gas?

Ride motorcycles! Ride horses! Get off your lazy asses and walk! But please...for the love of all that is holy, wear clothes when you do these things!

In a world without Don LaFontaine... (2008-09-02 09:28)

movie previews, and commercials won't be quite as much fun...

Voice Legend, Don LaFontaine has passed away.

I just loved the GEICO commercial where he showed just how seriously he took himself by making fun of himself.

R.I.P. Don and thanks...

On eBay and S&H (2008-09-02 10:58)

I remember a time when S &H meant Green Stamps...but I digress (so soon, you ask?)

Recently, I've been putting a few items up for sale on eBay, and doing a bit of shopping as well. Most, and I say most sellers are pretty reasonable in the Shipping and handling charges they ask for. Buy a few old magazines/comic books/paperback and you're not typically going to get reamed. Buy some DVD's and it's almost the same story.

Buy a CD and you're screwed. Bent over a barrel and (you get the idea), so a $2 CD ends up costing you $8 as they charge you $5.99 for S &H. Then the seller turns around and ships it Media Mail and pockets the difference. A single CD typically runs around $1.85 to send Media Mail. you want to charge me $2.50 or $3.00 to cover the cost of the envelope (better be padded) and a trip to the post office, I'm fine with that. Just don't try to get me thinking I'm saving money, when you're making money on so-called shipping and handling charges.

With the new Seller Feedback setup in place, I'm going to be letting sellers know when I think that shipping charges are too high. Heck, eBay even TELLS you when they think that S &H costs are too high...

GRRRRRR......

4000 Pounds of Bananas! (2008-09-03 10:14)

A terrific song by Harry Chapin, BTW...

I am in the process of cleaning out the comic collection, getting rid of the stuff that doesn't fit in my collection parameters. So far, I've had pretty good luck selling off a good chunk of my goal. Yesterday, for example, I hauled the contents of this shopping cart to the local grocery store. They are a post office substation, and do media mail shipping. The total weight of the comics I sent to one guy was over 120 pounds. That, my friends, is a lot of comic books/magazines/comic related stuff.

Music Meme (2008-09-03 10:21)

Word associations: You tell us what musical, band/artist, song, album etc each word makes you think of:

- Technology: Styx -Mr. Roboto
- Exercise: Bill Conti -Theme from 'Rocky'
- Punch: Carl Douglas -Kung Fu Fighting
- Temperature: Foriegner -Cold as Ice (or Rolling Stones -She's So Cold)
- Fire: Sprinsteen -Fire (he wrote it, Pointer Sisters had the hit...Boss's version is...hotter!) Clothes: ZZ Top -Sharp Dressed Man
- Doll: Buddy Knox -Party Doll
- Sweet: Anything by The Carpenters (as in Sticky sweet)
- Makeup: Anything by Culture Club or KISS or Hair Bands...especially Poison...who had better makeup than most women I've known.
- Drunk: Charlie Daniels Band -Drinkin' My Baby Goodbye

My thanks to [*LJ User: joncwriter*] for this inspiration...and he kyped it from someplace else!

A Question for the Ladies (2008-09-03 21:26)

There have been some women who have wondered when Sarah Palin is going to have the time to spend with her children if she's elected Vice President. Most men wouldn't dare ask that question because no matter the validity of the question, it's not a question a man can ask. Not a complaint, just an observation.

So, does it bother anyone but me that nobody asks that question of Barrack Obama? Is that because the assumption is that Michelle will take care of them?

The inequality of the question, who can ask the question and the fact that should even BE a question is very bothersome to me.

And I didn't need Mayor Rudy to bring this up...I happened to come up with this idea all by my Neanderthal-ic, testosterone ridden lonesome. ;-)

Release the Hounds! (2008-09-04 07:12)

Sarah Palin described herself as a Hockey Mom. Then she asked, "What's the difference between a Hockey Mom and a Pit Bull?"

Her answer? "Lipstick"

She said it herself. She's a pit bull unleashed on the Obama's. Her speech last night was so loaded with veiled and outright threats about what could happen if Obama is elected President. She not only mocked the Senator, but she was condescending to anyone who would support him. And the racial innuendo? It fairly seeped out of my speakers last night. That crack about how small town people are "always proud of their country" was a direct slap at Michelle Obama. She was talking about HER experience as a black woman. This is just the GOP's way of playing bait and switch and making it some bogus Patriotism bullshit.

Sarah Barracuda, indeed. Since she threw down the gauntlet with such venom and force, nobody can accuse any Democrat who goes after her of attacking a woman. She's her own security force.

V.P. debate should be interesting.

Writer's Block: Sharing Haikus (2008-09-05 12:17)

LJ Question: The Japanese haiku poet Basho once wrote, "Old pond / a frog jumps / the sound of water." Try writing some of your own haikus about the little things in your life. A haiku generally consists of a five syllable line, a seven syllable line and a second five syllable line, or you can use any ten to fourteen syllables.

A Box of Comics
On a sunny afternoon
Pure reading pleasure

* * * *

Republican Lies
Old McCain in the vanguard
Palin on the leash

* * * *

LiveJournal Questions
Are oftentimes quite lacking
This ain't one of those

* * * *

Friendship seldom dies
Sometimes it slumbers deeply
Others just drowsing

Writer's Block: The X-Files Birthday (2008-09-10 10:18)

LJ Question: Today in 1993, The X-Files first premiered. What's your favorite episode? Have you ever experienced paranormal activity yourself?

Why would anyone assume that I have a favorite episode?

I never watched the show. The truth may be "out there" but I found the show's premise to be "out there"

Flash Fiction Story (2008-09-10 12:24)

I wrote this over the course of a couple of weeks. I would prefer to write fiction, but it's just so hard for me to do. Poetry is just so much easier for me to write, even if I can't read much at one sitting.

Anyhow, here's the story I wrote. It clocks in at a stately 753 words...so it shouldn't take long. I would appreciate any feedback, especially specific comments about how to make it better. I'm considering entering this in a flash fiction contest.

=================

Soul Survivor

Simpson awoke with a start. The stench of blood and death hung like a shroud in the morning fog. Simpson tried to sit up only to find the charred remains of his friend Griffin lying across his torso.

With a heavy sigh and sense of regret, he gently moved his friends remains and got up. The fog made seeing very problematic, so his training took over. Finding his weapon and checking the clip, Simpson started a search, working out from where he awoke in small concentric circles.

All he found was death. The result of last nights ambush and counter-attack were strewn all over the clearing and into the trees. The remains of violence that had expended itself littered the ground in small islands of testimony to Man's savagery.

He found Rosenberger and one of the enemy where they had bayoneted one another. It appeared that Rosenberger took some time to die. Tucker wasn't far away, having taken three of the enemy before dying of blood loss. Each discovery felt like a blow to his soul.

Simpson literally stumbled across what was left of Lammers and Reid. He found it ironic that two men who could barely stand each other in life would die together trying to save each other. Simpson started to weep at their failure. Another shot.

He wanted to cry out, his panic at finding no survivors beginning to press in on him. Discipline prevailed for the moment but the hold was tenuous at best.

He found Barger; dead...Mullaney; dead...Kirby; dead...Kane; dead...and when he found Matt "Bubba, Boom Boom" Baker, he lost it. That was all of them. All dead. All the enemy were all dead as well. It surrounded him; crushing him; hammering at him like a rain of body blows.

All dead, save for him who was unscathed. Bloodied, dirtied, surrounded by death, pressing in on him from all sides, Simpson recalled the ferocity of last nights fighting. How it devolved into savage one on one combat, take no prisoners, just survive.
Which is what he did. He survived. Alone. As the reality of the situation settled on him, a piece of him died inside.

He found the report book. Wrote out the account of the fight as best he could then turned his attention to burial. Each of his compatriots were placed in a separate grave, clearly marked and with great care. The enemy, Simpson tossed in a shallow trench that he barely covered.

He felt drained. Mentally, physically and spiritually. The latter most of all. He found it almost surprising that this was so. He'd joined the service with the notion of protecting King and Country. He'd found that in a practical sense, that wasn't much of something to get worked up over fighting for. It sounded good, but he really found that he was fighting for his friends. The men he lived with, fought with and against, played cards with, laughed and cut up with and sometimes hated. The concept of fighting for you home, and the ideals that it stood for is better in thought, than practice. It's not the first thing that comes to mind when under attack.

Mechanically, he found some rations and began to eat. Leaning against a tree, he surveyed the battlefield, smelling the death, blood and failure. Hopelessness, bitterness and outrage at the waste of..."all of this!" flooded him and died quickly. His spirit was overwhelmed with the loss of his friends, his fellow soldiers and the senseless way everyone died. For what?
He was weary before the ambush last night. So were the men of his

squad. His brothers in arms, his friends. Everyone was so dog tired and worn out. Fighting to live another day, and now his friends battles were all over. Nobody really won this particular fight. It was all such as waste.

As he contemplated this, he mechanically ate what he could find amongst the debris of the battle. His melancholy overwhelming him, he slipped into a fitful doze, then a much deeper sleep.

*****

"Sarge!" hollered Corporal Selegue. "Sarge! Over here! It's Simpson!"

Sergeant Sargent hustled over to his corporal to see what he had found.

What he found was Simpson, under the tree apparently resting. He reached out to nudge him awake, and Simpson tumbled to the right. It was apparent to Sargent that Simpson was dead.

"Sarge? How do you think he died? There isn't a mark on him..."

Sargent just shook his head because he had no answer to that.

Writer's Block: 9/11 (2008-09-11 09:30)

**LJ Question: What were you doing on September 11th, 2001?
How do the events of that day hold meaning for you now?**

I was dropping off my wife at work that morning, when we heard Paul Harvey mention in the closing segment of his newscast that a plane had crashed into the World Trade Center. I found myself immediately wondering if it was a similar type of thing as the plane that crashed into the Empire State Building years ago. We now know the answer to that one. We knew it the minute the second plane went hurtling into the unhurt tower. We got that jolt every time the footage was shown. Over and over again. A body blow is sort of what it felt like to me.

I remember the news web sites being so hammered by people wanting information that they crashed. CNN.com was almost inaccessible for several hours. Then it was just bare bones. Same with ABC/CBS/NBC and so forth. I ended up listening to EPSN Radio because they canned sports broadcasting for the day and went to news. This was a national tragedy.

I was proud of our country in the days that followed. Silently, flags just started flying everywhere you looked. We weren't anything but Americans for the next few weeks. It was a nice feeling while it lasted. Then the jingoism and war mongering started, while some people wanted to step back and try and make sense of the tragedy and find the real culprits. There was this incredible surge to "Do Something" even if it was wrong, or so it seemed.

In the years that have followed, I have come to believe that Bush Jr. wanted to invade Iraq prior to 9/11 and that he used this as a gift wrapped chance to do so. There's compelling evidence this is so. Which is why I tend to dismiss out of hand the notion that we can't leave Iraq without it appearing we are running away. That there would be no victory. I find it hard to find victory in what appears to me to be an occupation.

People talk about the tarnish the US reputation has on it world wide since the start of the so-called 'War on Terror." One only has to read a bit about how the bulk of the Middle East views us to realize that we are totally without credibility in the region. Go ahead and read this article in the International Herald Tribune to see for yourself. It's pretty sad, to be honest.

I view 9/11 as one of the great tragedies to strike out country. I view the wrong headed reactions by the dubiously elected President, his advisors and lap dogs, and the ignorant masses who don't bother to actually learn anything about what's really going on as a tragedy of epic proportions that will shape, affect and cloud our country for years to come.

I never considered myself an reactionary. I never considered myself somebody who would get this up in arms over politics. 9/11 and the actions our country engaged in around the world have made me such. I was against the War in Iraq from the get-go. I thought it was about oil at the time, and little has happened to change my opinion.

I honor the memory of those who died in the Twin Towers, those who worked hard to find survivors, those who got sick due to the lack of leadership shown by Mayor Rudy in making sure all safety precautions were followed, and those who lost so much on that horrible day. I am shamed by the stupid notion that being a patriot means backing an illegal and immoral war. I love my country as much as they do, but I am saddened by what our so-called leaders have done in the name of "freedom."

Flash Fiction Story, Revised (2008-09-11 11:21)

Here's the revisions I've made. I'm sure there are grammatical, spelling, punctuation and other errors. Again, any thoughts or insight would be appreciated...

* * * * * * * * * *

Simpson awoke with a start. The stench of blood and death hung like a shroud in the morning fog. Simpson tried to sit up only to find the charred remains of his friend Griffin lying across his torso.

With a heavy sigh and sense of regret, he gently moved his friends remains and got up. The fog made seeing very problematic, so his training took over. Finding his weapon and checking the ammunition, Simpson started a search, working out from where he awoke in small concentric circles.

All he found was death. The result of last nights ambush and counter-attack were strewn all over the clearing and into the trees. The remains of violence littered the ground in small islands, testimony to Man's savagery.

He found Rosenberger and one of the enemy where they had bayoneted each another. It appeared that Rosenberger took some time to die. Tucker wasn't far away, having taken three of the enemy with him before blood loss did him in. Each discovery felt like a blow to his soul.

Simpson stumbled across what was left of Lammers and Reid. He found it ironic that two men who could barely stand each other in life, would die trying to save each other. Simpson started to weep at their failure. Another shot to his soul.

He wanted to cry out, his panic at finding no survivors beginning to press in on him. Discipline prevailed for the moment,, but the hold was tenuous at best.

He found Barger; dead...Mullaney; dead...Kirby; dead...Kane; dead...and when he found Matt "Bubba, Boom Boom" Baker, he lost it. That was all of them. All dead. All the enemy were all dead as well. It surrounded him; crushing him; hammering at him like a rain of body blows.

All dead, save for him and he was unscathed. Bloodied, dirtied, surrounded by death, pressing in on him from all sides, Simpson recalled the ferocity of the fighting last night. How it devolved into savage one on one combat. Take no prisoners. Just survive.

Which is what he did. He survived. Alone. As the reality of the situation settled on him, another piece of him died inside.

He found the report book. Wrote out the account of the fight as best he could then turned his attention to clean up. Simpson brought his compatriots together, covering them as best as he could, knowing that the army would come and collect their remains later. The enemy he left as they were. He had nothing to spare for them.

He felt drained. Mentally, physically and spiritually. The latter most of all. He found it almost surprising that this was so. He'd joined the service with the notion of protecting King and Country. He'd found that in a practical sense, that wasn't much of something to get worked up over fighting for. It sounded good, but he really found that he was fighting for his friends. The men he lived with, played cards with, laughed and cut up with, fought with and against and sometimes hated. The concept of fighting for your home, and the ideals that it stood for is better in thought, than practice. It's not the first thing that comes to mind when under attack.

Leaning against a tree, he surveyed the scene of the carnage, smelling the death, blood and failure. Hopelessness, bitterness and outrage at the waste of..."all of this!" flooded him and died quickly. His spirit was overwhelmed with the loss of his friends, his fellow soldiers and the senseless way everyone died. For what?

He was weary before the ambush last night. So were the men of his squad. His brothers in arms, his friends. Everyone was so dog tired and worn out. Fighting to live another day, and now his friends battles were all over. Nobody really won this particular fight. It was all so...depressing.

As he contemplated this, he mechanically ate what he had found amongst the debris of the battle. His melancholy consuming him, and the damp chill of the day seeming to seep into his bones, he wrapped himself up in his blanket. With that, he slipped into a fitful doze, followed by a much deeper sleep.

*****

"Sarge!" hollered Corporal Selegue. "Sarge! Over here! It's Simpson!"

Sergeant Sargent hustled over to his corporal to see what he had found. They had been looking for this squad for a day. When they didn't report, it made everyone at HQ uneasy.

What he found was Simpson, under the tree apparently resting. He reached out to nudge him awake, and Simpson tumbled to the right. It was apparent to Sargent that Simpson was dead.

"Sarge? How do you think he died? There isn't a mark on him..."

Sargent just shook his head because he had no answer.

Writer's Block: Missing from Nature (2008-09-12 11:29)

LJ Question: If one thing were to be stricken from nature, what could you stand to see go?

Festering anger. It really is pretty useless.

Writer's Block: Independence Day (2008-09-16 12:52)

LJ Question: In recognition of Mexican Independence Day, tell us how you celebrate your own independence.

This reminds me that no matter what I think, I am not my own[1]. Therefore, I can't celebrate my own independence. Were I to, I would just end up in a whirl of doo-doo... Been there, done that...lost the ferschluggin' t-shirt (and I don't want it back)

1. 1 Corinthians 6:20 - For you have been bought with a price: therefore glorify God in your body. (NAS)

So, I've got a problem (2008-09-19 09:37)

I am a baseball fan of the highest order. Most times, if there's a ball game on TV, I'll be watching. Doesn't matter who plays, just want to watch the game. Heck, I even watch the Cubs on occasion (don't root for them though...that would be bad).

I'm also a huge Green Bay Packer fan. Neither of these admissions should come as a surprise to long time readers of this here LJ...

The problem, you ask? What to do on Sunday Night!!!

Y'see, the New York Yankees play their last game EVER at Yankee Stadium Sunday night and the game is on ESPN. The Packers, with new QB Aaron Rodgers play 'Merica's Team (yarite), the Dallas Cowpokes on NBC at the same time.

What's a man to do? I don't want to spend the whole night channel flippin' as that wears your average couch potato out...but WAUGH!!!!

I am so confused...

MoKan! (What's a MoKan, Mommie?) (2008-09-22 12:18)

8:48 A.M. found me on the Gold Wing, zipping along I-70, somewhere between Columbia and Concordia, MO, the Brian Setzer Orchestra is a gonna "Rock This Town" and they are blaring their intentions out of the speakers as I was heading to Kansas City to go to the MoKan Comics Conspiracy (which is about the dumbest name for a convention I've every heard in all my born days...). The black-eyed susans littered the side of the highway scenery, combined with a few smaller trees with leaves turning red, made for some pleasant visuals down the road. The lack of rain, and bountiful sunshine also contributed.

Besides the funny book show, I was also going to see friend Eric, meet his friend Matt, and also be able to see Eric's charming and long suffering wife, Sarah and their two little boys. I wheeled into Eric's driveway, stowed my motorcycle stuff, changed shoes, and away we went. I learned from last year that engineer boots on concrete for several hours can be wearisome on my feet. I started throwing money at dealers almost immediately upon arrival, using my handy-dandy nerdy checklist to fill holes in my collection. Very quickly, I filled one of the reusable grocery sacks I brought from home. So, I felt the need to empty it out in Eric's car, and go back in to refill it. Which I did, thank you.

In between bargain hunting, I spent some time being a geek and hanging around the comics creators (writers and artists). Sergio Aragones and the entire Groo Crew were there. I've never read any Groo. It just never appealed to me. But I have read some other stuff that Aragones wrote, so I stopped by to tell him how much I enjoyed the recent Bat Lash series, and his work on The Spirit. Since the Spirit is something of a sacred cow of mine, comics wise, he had to be doing a good job. I even had my picture taken with Sergio!

I have to admit that going through long boxes of comics, or digging through bargain bins, sort of makes me feel like a bit of a dumpster diver. Especially in a Convention setting. But, with all the nifty bargains I picked up, I shouldn't complain. Eric found some things he was looking for, including a small ton of comics for his not quite 2 year old son. The little guy sits there and lets you read the whole darn comic book to him. Apparently, he's riveted to them. Which is a good thing. Should help him learn to read on his own and appreciate the beauty of sequential art as a medium for telling stories.

Meeting Matt and his family was a real treat. Matt is a friend of Eric's from Eric's Karate Club, and both are members of the KirbyKomics ~~Group of Yahoo's~~, I mean Yahoo Group that I belong to, so that made for an interesting and fun get together. My only regret is that Matt and family couldn't join us for dinner at this nifty German place in Independence. A place called the Rheinland Restaurant and you know what? I TRIED THE VEAL!!!

That's right! I wasn't there all week, I did tip the waitress, and I tried the Veal! Jagerschnitzel, to be exact. Und it vas gutt! (Comic book German for ya, right there). It was served with a side of Spatzle, and the whole thing was great. Had I not been looking at a 120 mile ride home, I would've had some yummy dark German beer in a bucket big enough to dive in. Alas, keeping what few wits about me whilst piloting the Gold Wing home won out, so I had Apple Cider instead.

Visiting with Eric and Sarah and getting a little caught up with them, in between paying attention to the kids was lots of fun. I always enjoy seeing them and spending time with them. I have got to get Elaine to go with me to the Rheinland. She won't try the veal, but they have plenty of other stuff I believe she'd like.

The ride home was uneventful, which is a good thing. I did realize that I had conflicted perspectives, often at the same moment. Or so it seemed...I would look at the odometer, and marvel at how much ground I covered in what I thought was a short time. I was going to get home so much sooner than I had originally thought. Yay me! Then again, I'd immediately think, I've still got so far to go! I'll never get home! WAUGH!

I made it home in good time, hugged Elaine mightily (because I missed her) and pretty well collapsed in a tired puddle on the floor. I'm getting too old for this sort of stuff. :-)

I'm a voter and I'm tired of this message (2008-09-22 22:13)

I don't know about you, but I am more than a little tired of the phrase, "I'm (politician of your choice) and I approve this message." Especially when they did all the speaking in the ferschluggin' commercial in the first darn place!!! I mean, it's not like the Swift Boat Veterans for ~~Lies~~ Truth are doing the talking for you, when you're doing your own ad!

Get over yourselves and THINK a little. How bloody stupid do you sound approving your own message, anyhow? I wish to heck it wasn't so widespread, or I'd use it as criteria to not vote for you.

Idiots...

Oh yeah, I'm the writer of this piece, and I approve this message (doesn't that sound dumber than a pork chop?)

A Question (2008-09-26 21:07)

It's my understanding that many people are against any sort of bailout of Wall Street and the current financial crisis. Let them stew in their own Greedy Juices, or so the feeling goes.

It appears is this the will of the people. That's fine. But...what if they're wrong? And as a result we end up with a financial disaster equal to or worse than the Great Depression?

Jus' wonderin'

(On the road in Ohio...and onto Canada...)

Writer's Block: R.E.A.D. in America Day (2008-09-27 20:24)

LJ Question: In celebration of R.E.A.D. in America Day, tell us about what you're reading. How is reading important to you? What would you recommend to others?

I've been on a real funny book kick. Reading comics like I was 12 years old again. It's been great.

Amongst the 4 color madness have been a couple of modern day pulp novels. Collected together between two covers, a pair of Max Allen Collins Nolan books, with the collection called "Two for the Money." It was plot/character driven genre fiction, and great brain candy. If you like that sort of thing, that is. Roughly the equivalent to a good popcorn movie.

Reading is such a part of who I am and what I enjoy doing. I can't imagine a world without books, and my life without books. In fact, we had a little time alone here in Kitchener, Ontario and we took some time to do our part to help the local economy and buy some books from a used book store right across the street from the hotel we're staying in.

So, in that sense, we took R.E.A.D. in America Day, International!

On the road in Canada...

Time to go home (2008-09-29 08:15)

After spending the past couple of days in Canada, it is now time to start the long trip home.

Will post more about the trip later...

Traveling Eats (2008-10-02 09:04)

I like to eat. Take a look at any picture of me taken in the past 15 years and you'll notice that my waist has been expanding. Food is something I enjoy. A lot. Probably too much, to be honest...
We returned from a trip to Canada to see family and to attend the Installation service of my cousin, the Reverend Robert Bugbee, as President of the Lutheran Church of Canada this past Sunday. I'll write more about that later.

Right now, I wanna talk about food. Food I ate whilst I was gone away from home and the comforts of said home stomping grounds. I tried many new things, including Rouladen, Curried Goat and Wiener schnitzel (and no, they weren't using Schnauzer...). I would not hesitate to eat any of them again. My aunt fixed up the Rouladen and used us as guinea pigs. I'll be her culinary Guinea Pig any ol' day...

That is a picture of my wonderful Aunt Vi, and her Rouladen. Needless to say, we had a marvelous meal. Another surprise was her cooked carrots. I've never liked cooked carrots, as I've always preferred them raw. However, she did something sneaky good with them, such as cooking them in chicken broth with a touch of sugar. Yum. Gotta try that at home. Actually, gonna try that at home...

As good as the meal was, being able to sit down to dinner with my Aunt, her husband, my Dad and his wife, Grandma Stratton and my own wonderful wife, that was the best. Hands down, the best. Even though I've managed at various points in my life to do my darnedest to mess up my family relationships, that they still love and forgive me is amazing.
The night before we had this marvelous dining experience, three of us (Grandma, Elaine and I) trundled off to Al Smith's in Toledo. I like the place as the food is basic, and always good. But they have this desert that is simply to die for. I mean, it is that good. I shied away from bread pudding for years because the crap they labeled as such in the school cafeteria was of the consistency of rubber and were I ever to actually try to eat road kill, I'm fairly certain that this is what it would taste like. Al Smith's Bread Pudding is something altogether different. It requires a small dinner in front of it, because they serve it to you in a soup bowl. Or a salad bowl, or a bowl large enough to go swimming in. As you can see from the photo, it's ginourmously huge

I mean, we're not talking any wimpy serving sizes here now are we kids? No sirree, this is desert for the healthy appetite. And I do believe they slip some actual whiskey in the sauce that is drizzled (poured?) over it. All I know is that when I'm done, I have this warm glow...and want to take a nap.

And the other noteworthy culinary adventure entailed trying out a new fast food place on the way up north. This stop in Indiana was at a place called Skyline Chili. I'd seen the signs, heard some comments from I forget where, so decided with the consent of my wife, to give it a whirl. While I enjoyed the food, I thought it was rather expensive and not worth a return visit. However, I did note that they used a LOT of cheese on the items I ordered.

Which was a Chili 4 Way (above) and Coney's (below). There really is food under the cheese. One last note about Skyline Chili...if the waitress offers you a bib? Take one and use it....

So, I like food. Thanks to my sister, I have developed a liking for taking pictures of my food. I try not to wear my food, but sometimes it happens. Oh yeah, never forget to Try the Veal!

Writer's Block: Day of German Unity (2008-10-03 07:02)

LJ Question: It's the Day of German Unity, marking the 1990 reunification of East and West Germany. In our current period of global instability, do you ever feel nostalgic for the seeming simplicity of the Cold War?

Oh yeah, that feeling that if some crazy idiot near a button could launch Nuclear (not Nuke-U-Lar) Armageddon...is something I really miss. About like I'd miss a good case of The Clap, a toothache, or being suffocated by a demented super-villain.

Debate, Schmebate (2008-10-03 08:08)

Open note to the McCain campaign...

I have seldom been so insulted in my voting life. Having Gubbner Palin state outright that she weren't a gonna answer the questions the way they wuz done being asked, or ta suit da Media Elite (like she could even spell that), was a slap in da face of smart 'Mericans everywhere...

Ok, enough of that stuff...I really was insulted watching the so-called debate last night. It was an exercise in The Mantra, and an attack on anyone who dares to think a bit outside the box. It's glaringly apparent that Ms. Palin is a Washington outsider. She's a tool, albeit an attractive tool of the Republican Party. People that buy into her "aw shucks" are suckers. We've gotten into the current mess with people who aren't Intellectually Elite. Thanks, but I'd rather have somebody smarter than me manning the controls.

You did you handlers proud, Ms. Palin. You ducked serious questions, didn't make yourself out to be a complete idiot, gave the vague impression that you knew what you were talking about, even if you didn't address the questions asked. Other than that, you really insulted my intelligence. And I'm not any smarter than you. Nice job...

Book Review - <u>Dime Novel Desperadoes: The Notorious Maxwell Brothers</u> (2008-10-03 09:40)

I couldn't finish it. This book was written with excuses for the bad behavior exhibited by the Maxwell Brothers. The psychological bombs were being dropped from the very beginning of the book, rather than focusing on telling the story, offering the authors conclusions at the end of the book. This makes for an annoying read, to be honest. Don't try and tell me what to believe, lay out the facts, show me why you came to the conclusions you did, but leave me to arrive at my own conclusions by myself.

This is really sad for me to say. I'm the target audience of books like this. I enjoy reading about the Old West, and the cover of this book promised much. So did the advertising blurbs. Too bad the author didn't or couldn't deliver. His research was solid, although he tended to use the phrase "almost certainly" or variations on that ad nauseum. It became clear to me that this was a writing crutch that a good editor should have shot down as over used.

This is flawed history and biography, at best. At worst, it's insulting to anyone with a modicum of intelligence. Show, don't tell. Avoid this piece of clap trap like the plague.

A copy of this book was provided by the publisher for the purpose of this review.

Concert List (2008-10-06 09:29)

The following is a list of artists/bands I have seen in concert. I used to think my taste was pretty eclectic, but looking at this list, I need to get out more...

Bob Seger & The Silver Bullet Band
The Rockets (from Detroit)
Ted Nugent
Asia
Loverboy
Donnie Iris
Bryan Adams
Journey
REO Speedwagon
Moody Blues
Marshall Tucker Band
.38 Special
Outlaws
Black Sabbath
Pat Travers Band
Toad the Wet Sprocket
Shiny Toy Guns
Crowded House
Glenn Miller Band
B.B. King
L'il Ed & Dave Weld
Loretta Lynn
Conway Twitty
Randy Travis
Vern Gosdin
Alabama
Lee Greenwood
Eddy Raven
Ricky Van Shelton
Reba McEntire
Holly Dunn
Charlie Daniels Band
Kathy Mattea
Philip Glass
Bill Cosby
Billie Jo Spears
Asleep at the Wheel
The Bellamy Brothers
Joe Diffie

Highway 101
Patty Loveless
Statler Brothers
George Jones
Jerry Reed
Liam Finn
16 Frames

McCain has no honor (2008-10-06 11:49)

I read with interest and listened to the talking heads bloviate about how the McCain campaign has stated that it's going to go after Obama, dispensing with The Issues and indulging in character assassination. Governor Palin already started by trying to desperately link Obama to a terrorist who he has crossed paths with. My question for her would be, what did she expect him to do? Sock him in the nose? Spit in his face? Knee him in the groin and stomp on him?

Maybe in Moose Hunting land, but not in the real world.

We all run across characters in life who are less than ideal. Everyone does. That's just a stone fact. What matters is how you deal with them. He denounced the activities of this guy, and pointed out that when all this terrorism went on, he was 8 years old.

McCain has no honor anymore. He has shown he's willing to sell his soul to the devil to win. That the "anything goes" mentality is what he'll adopt when it appears he's losing. So, sit back and get ready for a mass of cheap shots and out and out lies. With the Pit Bull Hockey Mom around to spew faux patriotic drivel and look the fool she may or may not be...this should show the American People what their true choices are.

Oh, and where is Palin's flag pin? Why does she hate America? ;-)

Good for Goose, Good for the Gander
(Guest Post) (2008-10-08 09:25)

On the Yahoo Group (KirbyKomics) that I have mentioned before, friend and author Van Reid posted the following. With his kind and gracious permission, I pass it along here. I found much food for thought.

——

Some time ago I read something written by Al Capp; I can't recall where or when. He talked (I think to an interviewer) about how he had flogged the political right for years, but decided that the hippy left in the sixties were ripe for satire. What struck him was that when he burst the political bubble of the right or caricatured a right wing politician, they often wrote to him asking for the original which they would hang proudly in their office. When he started to satirize the hippy left (with a peacenik named Joanie Phonie and the like), he was threatened with law suits and received letters telling him he was being offensive and mean.

This has always stuck with me and my experience with Eastern liberals (or perhaps I should say Northeastern liberals) is that they lack the ability to laugh at themselves. One reason Maggie and I (independently, before we knew each other) both got out of the anti-nuclear cause was that the people around us considered anyone who disagreed with them as either stupid or evil. This is where I first saw what I think of as leftist fundamentalism and I have seen an awful lot of it since.

I have said before, I am not a right winger or a hawk. I think of myself as an old-fashioned conservative, which is not the opposite or mutually exclusive to being liberal. It simply means moderate, thoughtful, as liberal means open-minded and forgiving. So I am not espousing a "political" point of view (I hardly have one these days), just putting a thought out there.

I just read a short and dismissive review of "An American Carol" in the New York Times. "Cheap shots and mean-spirits abound" says the reviewer. Now this is not a movie that sounded promising to me, but I wonder why satirizing the left is any more an indication of cheap shots or mean spiritedness than say Stewart and Colbert or Bill Mahar's new movie about religion – all of which are lauded in the New York Times as being funny and witty. If the movie isn't funny, so be it, but that's just a failure of humor not an indication that the targets are any less deserving than Stewart's. It's okay to satirize the right, but mean-spirited to satirize the left? Some of the shots on the comedy shows are at extremely easy targets. Who's any easier a target than Bush, for goodness sakes. The guy can hardly talk!

I don't think the "left" (a political entity) is doing liberalism (a social good) any favors by taking itself so seriously. Maybe others see less of this leftist fundamentalism where you live. (Rightist fundamentalism is well documented.) These are just quick thoughts off the top of my head and suspecting that someone here will have something about this that will be well worth reading.

—

Again, thanks to Van for his permission to reprint this here. I'd be interested in thoughts you might have.

Writer's Block: Personal Holidays (2008-10-08 09:54)

LJ Question: These days, there's a holiday for everything from punctuation to pie. If you could create your own holiday, what would it be and how would you celebrate?

I would probably create a holiday that is free from holidays. A day that would be like a normal Thursday was, 24 years ago. Nothing special going on, no cards to buy or mail, no big dinner to fix, go to, or bail out of. A day that begins quietly, continues quietly and concludes quietly. No fireworks, no speeches, no cute magnetic ribbons on cars, or door decorations.

I'm probably not the only person to come up with this, but I am tired of being Holiday Marketed to death.

That is all.

Writer's Block: The Beatles (2008-10-09 14:45)

**LJ Question: In their heyday, The Beatles were the center of the pop universe. Many groups have been hailed as the next Beatles, but does pop music even have a center anymore?
Who represents the core of pop music to you?**

I don't think there is a center of the Pop universe anymore, because there isn't a cultural center any more. We have so many more choices now, so many narrowly programmed radio stations, cable channels and the like. It's quite possible to have artists who are quite popular that you've never heard of.

Diversity has taken hold in ways nobody imagined, I'll bet. Which is kind of cool, yet sort of sad in a way. Only because there are generations of people who won't have the pop cultural glue to hold them together. The shared things like TV Shows, due to the chance to duck out of watching something because something else is on TV or the 'Net or in the Game Console.

Writer's Block: Live Music (2008-10-10 10:59)

LJ Question: When it comes to bebop, you want to take it straight, no chaser. And a smoky jazz club is the best place to get it. What's your favorite kind of place to see live music?

Where there are live people, thanks.

My Fellow Citizens (2008-10-13 11:01)

I address this to My Fellow United State Citizens primarily.

I have been following this past weeks Presidential Campaign with a mixture of horror and sadness. Not to mention some basic anger. Allow me to explain why I feel this way, what has caused me to feel this way and how we can pull back from the political and societal abyss we are edging ever closer to.

I heard the Talking Heads on a couple of Cable News Channels hammering away at some of the McCain and Palin rallies where the roiling anger at the distinct possibility that Obama may win the election next month cause some of my fellow citizens to act in horribly inappropriate ways. Cat calls to "Kill Him" and cries of "Terrorist" and "Traitor" were just a couple of the more extreme reactions. Calls for McCain to "Fight!" Obama, and the by now famous clip of that poor, misinformed woman saying that she had read that Obama was "an Arab" like that was a "BAD THING!"

Kudos to McCain for taking the time, the chance and the opportunity to not only correct the woman, but to point out something of great value. Namely, that Obama is a decent man. A family man. A fellow citizen like McCain and his supporters. That he just disagrees with him on basic, fundamental issues. For his efforts, he got booed. By his own supporters. Dollars to doughnuts, he also lost votes from people in that room, and around the country.

There is nothing wrong with disagreeing with somebody. That's the nature of discussion and the basis of the give and take called compromise. Somewhere along the line, we as a country have lost sight of that. We have bought into the notion that complete and total victory is the only acceptable outcome. This has lead to members of our political parties, the talking heads on TV, columnists in the paper and Talk Radio pundits to attack not only the views and positions of the opposition, but to belittle the person as well. After all, if the person who opposes you is made to look foolish, then their position by extension must also be foolish and we can just dismiss them completely.

This dismissive behavior, of which I am just as guilty, has brought our country low. We no longer have political discourse. We have brawls. We label the people we disagree with as
"EVIL" as if disagreeing with somebody makes a person evil. People have lost sight of what true evil is, and have cheapened the work and thus the concept of it. On the face of it, it equates somebody who honestly believes that abortion is wrong with some of the truly heinous people in world

history. I'm sorry, but believing that abortion is wrong doesn't make somebody as wretched or as big a waste of skin as Ted Bundy. Nor does believing that the Right to Choose to have an abortion make a person a horrific murderer or piece of scum along the lines of Jack the Ripper.

That's just beyond the pale of reasonable thought. Yet, it happens in everyday life. I have been asked, "What is WRONG with you?" for daring to disagree with several somebody's over my views on various topics. Since when does having a different opinion mean that I am somehow flawed as a person? That the entirety of my being and existence is somehow "wrong?" What about how I feel about other subjects and topics that we might agree on? Does my disagreement about one or two invalidate my entire personhood?

Somehow, I don't think so. Nor do most of you, no matter how strongly you believe in your own positions on things. However, we do it to each other all the time, both individually and collectively. I see it on LJ and elsewhere. Name calling, dismissive dialogue and out and out lies being told about each other. Doesn't matter at this point who started it. What matters is who has the Stones to end it. To talk to their supporters and tell them that treating the opposition with Respect and Dignity is the best, smartest and ultimately American way to do things.

For myself, I've had more than my fill of the Michael Moore's and Rush Limbaugh's of the world. The anti-social screeds of Al Franken and Michael Savage do little to actually accomplish anything. No, they actually contribute to the grid-lock in Congress and elsewhere. Because the goal of politics in the U.S. has changed from working out doable and helpful compromise to Ultimate Victory. At any cost! Compromise is no longer seen as honorable, but almost treacherous.

Poppycock, I tell you. It's not always in the best interest of the Lunatic Fringe (plenty on both sides of the aisle), but compromise is usually the best for the most people. As Winston Churchill once said, "It has been said that democracy is the worst form of government except all the others that have been tried." We must keep this in mind. The system that we have, while not perfect, is the best one going. It works best with mutual respect as the building block.

I urge the more civilized members of both parties and all political persuasions to tell the most vocal and extreme to not only tone it down, but to shut the hell up. If for no other reason than when something worth getting angry about happens, that people already accustomed to hearing the screaming won't tune it out as so much noise.

Finally, I'd like to urge you to not fall into the trap of thinking, "I will if they do." That's a zero sum game. That ensures that nothing changes. The best way to deal with obnoxious behavior and rhetoric is to challenge it politely but firmly. You simply must be better than the other person or persons. I realize this makes me appear naive and unrealistically hopeful. So be it. It can work if enough people get behind the idea. It's one that America is more than ready for.

iTunes Genius is only Pretty Smart (2008-10-15 09:20)

I've had mixed success with the new 'Genius' function in iTunes 8. Mainly because it is SO limited in what it will work with. Pretty much has to be mainstream music in order to work.

I used a song by April Wine as the 'seed' and had no trouble. I've tried at least a dozen songs by John Coltrane, Miles Davis, Dave Brubeck and get "Genius doesn't work with this song...blah, blah, blah..." Yet it works with Triumph, a middlin' band of minor note and a poor reflection of Rush. Somebody, please explain this to me.

[EDIT: All of this was done on my new iPod classic]

So, until 'Genius' gets smarter, let's just call it Pretty Smart/Limited

Buckley in the News (2008-10-15 11:23)

Regarding a Letter to my Fellow Citizens recently, I direct your attention to the following pieces on The Daily Beast:

[1]Sorry, Dad, I'm Voting for Obama
[2]Buckley Bows Out of National Review

The reactions by the Right (nor correct) that lead to his resignation, the calls of 'Betrayal' and the ugly suggestions as to what Kathleen's mother should have done with her, are a stellar, perfect example of what I was talking about.

Further, the remarks that John Lewis made last week are also an example of the over bearing and wrong headed rhetoric we've had too much of lately. I realize that we've come a long way from where we used to be, and that things have "always been this way." That doesn't mean we should put up with it or tolerate it.

It's okay to disagree without being disagreeable. Reagen and Tip O'Neill did it...and they were miles apart politically.

http://www.thedailybeast.com/blogs-and-stories/2008-10-10/the-conservative-case-for-obama/
http://www.thedailybeast.com/blogs-and-stories/2008-10-14/sorry-dad-i-was-fired

10 Years (2008-10-17 10:04)

I seldom struggle with words. They usually come pretty easy to me. There have been few times in my life when I've had to struggle to find the right words, the proper words, the words that will convey exactly what I want to say, to express the feelings in my head and in my heart.

This is one of those times.

Ten years ago, I married my best friend. She is without a doubt, one of the finest people I've ever known in my life. That she chose me, still baffles me. That she still smiles when I come home gladdens me more than I could ever express in words.

> *Whispers of grace flow from her smile,*
> *As she peers at me from across the room.*

I can't write love poetry to save my life. The first line I like…and is so true in her.

My faith is very important to me. It's a huge part of who I am. I have been so blessed to have as a partner in life such a good witness. Somebody who lives with such grace, her faith. It is an inspiration to me, and something that humbles me. She would argue with me about this, but that's my story and I am sticking to it.

Mainly because it's the truth about her as I see it. I remember her mother (God rest her soul) told me before we got married, "Well, life with Elaine won't be dull."

She was right. Life hasn't been dull with her. Smiles, laughs, giggles, and all sorts of fun things have followed over the past decade. Not moments of overwhelming drama, but entertaining and enjoyable. We've had our share of losses (both her parents and my mother and grandmother, plus the continued lack of my daughter's presence) but we've come through in good shape, by the Grace of G*d.

I thank Him, and I thank her. Love is a choice and one that takes courage on a daily basis. The alternative is easy and one I've taken as well. Running away from trouble or problems isn't in her makeup. I thank her for making that choice every day. I can honestly say that my life is a better place for her being such a major part of it, and that I would be lost without her.

The writer of Proverbs wrote in the 31st Chapter,

> **10** *A wife of noble character who can find? She is worth far more than rubies.*
> *She is a wife of noble character,*

and a lot of fun besides.

I love you, Elaine. Thank you for 10 great years. Looking forward to 10 more!

Writer's Block: Comedians as Journalists (2008-10-17 10:48)

LJ Question: Distrust of the media has grown to the point where many people only trust the news if it comes from a comedian. Who do you trust more: Stephen Colbert or Jon Stewart?

Walter Cronkite.

And that's the way it is...

Writer's Block: Cryptozoology (2008-10-21 10:26)

LJ Question: Bigfoot, the Yeti, the Loch Ness Monster, el chupacabra—what is your favorite creature that may or may not exist?

Honest, hard working Politicians...

This is disgusting (2008-10-21 15:18)

I am amazed at this story. From the KMBC story, the clerk didn't even have to type the offending words in, just select from a list. Why in the name of all that's Holy, would ANY company have that epithet as a choice? What color is the sky in their version of reality?

Boycott this chain of stores. They don't deserve your money or your patronage. Your absence at the cash registers will speak louder than anything else you could say.

clipped from www.kansascity.com

Report: Racial slur written on receipt

A 22-year-old Kansas City man says he found a racial slur printed on his receipt after returning a pair of shoes.

KMBC-TV reported today that customer Keith Slater bought the shoes last weekend from the Journeys shoe store at Oak Park Mall. A few days later he returned the shoes after finding a cheaper pair at another store.

Slater got his money back but it was not until later that he noticed Cust: Dumb followed by the N-word printed on the receipt.
The Slaters returned to the store the next day, but they said they never got a full explanation.

KMBC reported that no one at the store would talk about what happened, and that a spokesman with the Journeys corporate office would only say that the matter is being investigated.

ENOUGH! (2008-10-22 08:27)

I have been getting emails from people, who I'm sure are certain that WE ARE DOOMED if Obama is elected president. One suggested rather strongly that he is the Anti-Christ and the other stated that we were headed down the road of Socialism, with Hilary Clinton as a Supreme Court Justice to boot!

When did sending racist, borderline racist screeds and out right lies become acceptable? Especially to people you know who are too polite to tell you to go screw yourself and your damnable extremist political views? There are lines friends and family shouldn't cross. This is one of those lines. You want to talk politics with me, that's fine. Call me, or come to my house. Don't send me whack job emails. I don't care if you're a Rightie or a Leftie or a Commie Pinko...stay out of my inbox with that crap.

Oh, and don't you dare impugn my Patriotism or Love of Country by suggesting that if I don't forward something, I'm part of the problem.

Oh, for the love of Ol' Pete (2008-10-22 17:43)

This is just goofy...absolutely goofy. I gotta wonder what the British think of stuff like this. If they even care about stuff like this...read the whole article if interested....

> clipped from [1]news.bbc.co.uk
>
> **McCain in baseball election play**
>
> US Republican presidential candidate John McCain has accused his rival, Barack Obama, of supporting both teams playing in the baseball World Series.
>
> The baseball championship series begins on Wednesday, and both teams -the Tampa Bay Rays and the Philadelphia Phillies -are from key swing states.

Brett No Benedict Favre! (2008-10-22 17:50)

Well, this is beyond silly. Of course, if you consider the original source, and that nobody else has confirmed it...I think that tells you a lot right there.

'Nuff Said.

> *clipped from sports.espn.go.com*
>
> ### Favre says he didn't give Millen, Lions any inside info about Packers
>
> HAM PARK, N.J. – Brett Favre insists he's no Benedict Brett. The New York Jets quarterback denied reports that he called former Detroit president Matt Millen a few weeks ago and gave him and Lions coaches information they could use in a game against the Green Bay Packers.

Review: The Michael Stanley Band -Stage Pass
(2008-10-23 10:40)

The 1970's saw a flood, nay more like a tsunami of Live records after the left field success of Peter Frampton's "Frampton Comes Alive." Record companies fell all over themselves to get a live record out there by almost every artist on their rosters.

Most were unfortunate in that they sounded like the slap dash efforts they were. Too often, the recordings were a mess and had to be 'sweetened' in the studio later. In other words, they would use part of the live recording, and re-record other parts. Making them less live in actuality.

The Michael Stanley Band was one of the hardest working bands in the midwest during this time period. Rabid fans in their native Cleveland, Oh and environs helped them land a recording contract, and Epic/Columbia had them rush a live album out in response to the above mentioned album. As MSB were in the midst of recording their next studio album, some five tracks made their debut on Stage Pass, a double live LP release that nicely fits onto a single CD.

The gentle ballad "Rosewood Bitters" sounds quite nice in a live setting. The lead off track, "Midwest Midnight" is a angry attack on the music industry, and the first stanza is about Spanking the Monkey under the covers. Took me a long time to really figure that out...and the rockin' 'Strike Up the Band' closes out the album.

This release shows what a tight, solid band MSB was at that time. It shows why their stage show was justifiably popular and worth seeing. MSB is one of those groups that commonly gets labeled, "Should've made it bigger" and in this instance, I think it's a worthwhile label. Also, it's a worthwhile album to get. Lots of fun, and some great playing by a great band.

(note: In the original posting, there was a copy of the album cover. For copyright reasons, it didn't seem prudent to include it here.)

Review: The Detective & Mr. Dickens -William J. Palmer
(2008-10-23 11:51)

Certainly for more sexually explicit than one would imagine a book set in that time period, it is a cracking good story with many real people and events thrown in for good measure.

Palmer does tend to liberally use sensationalism for its own sake, and not to move the story along. My guess is that he wanted to illustrate that sexual depravity wasn't anything new. That even supposed upper class people were just as apt to be involved in perversion as anyone else.

Palmer's characters, as depicted in the book, were interesting and the use of the First Person narrative makes it seem like we are actually witnessing the same events as Wilkie, the teller of the tale. Worth a read, whether you are a fan of Dickens or not.

Local Radio Firings (2008-10-23 15:34)

I can't say that I'm surprised. We live in a college town, where cheap radio labor due to the Journalism School at Ol' Mizzou flows like water. Still, KFRU is probably going to lose me as a listener for most everything except Cardinal Baseball. The constant and repeated disregard for the community which it allegedly serves in these two firings is appalling.

I don't care for the politics of either man. They are both very conservative. But, they never made themselves out to be more than just what they were. They had their opinions and seldom crossed the line of stating that you were an idiot if you disagreed with them. Fred Parry often called Simon Rose an idiot, but most of the time, Rose was being an idiot.

I'll miss Claxton. He's been a part of my morning for some time. Since the two firings, and the constant carrying of Rush Limbaugh, I will sadly no longer be listening to KFRU in the morning. Or the afternoon, for that matter. It's things like this that make satellite radio look better and better.

clipped from www.columbiatribune.com

Tight economy cited in latest KFRU firing

By the Tribune's™ staff
Published on columbiatribune.com Thursday, October 23, 2008

KFRU News Director Dan Claxton was fired today, the second high-profile dismissal at the station this week. Fred Parry was fired from his position as co-host of the "Morning Meeting" program on Tuesday.

Claxton said John Walker, Cumulus marketing manager, informed him of the decision at about 9:30 a.m.

"I was told the economy was so tight that they just couldn't afford to keep me on," Claxton said, noting that his understanding is that Atlanta-based parent company Cumulus Media Inc. has directed stations to cut costs, and "I was one of those costs that got cut."

This is just plain stupid (2008-10-23 16:24)

I understand the anger. Really, I get it. Do a piss poor job running a large investment company or a bank, get a huge pile of cash as a parting gift after screwing the pooch on your way out the door pretty well equals instant anger in my book.

This ain't the way to handle that there anger, Boys and Girls. There are better, more mature ways of dealing with this sort of frustration. Call the Men and Women of the U.S. Congress, write letters, get them to make damn sure these knuckleheads don't get to leave their former places of employment with so much as a name plate, never mind a huge payoff or golden parachute. All sending bogus chemical threats does is get you labeled as a crank and not taken at all seriously.

People, we are better than this. C'mon...think!

clipped from www.cnn.com

'It's payback time,' banks warned in threat letters

WASHINGTON (CNN) --Letters containing white powder that were sent to more than 50 financial institutions warned that "it's payback time," the FBI said Thursday.

Officials said most of the powder-laced letters were sent to branches of JPMorgan Chase.
"Steal tens of thousands of people's money and not expect repercussions. It's payback time. What you just breathed in will kill you within 10 days. Thank [word redacted] and the FDIC for your demise," said one letter released by the FBI on Thursday.

Most of the letters contained a powder that the FBI said is harmless.

But sending the letters is "a serious crime," even if they are a hoax, FBI spokesman Richard Kolko said in a statement.

More than 50 letters were received this week at financial institutions in 11 states and the District of Columbia, the FBI said.

Writer's Block: The Final Frontier (2008-10-24 08:30)

LJ Question: Imagine a world without Star Trek. Is it a world you'd be very happy to live in, or a dark and terrible place?

I am unable to assess the situation, Captain. I do not have the necessary data to do so.

What a stupid question...

Dibbles, Meet the Dibbles... (2008-10-24 10:15)

My buddy Mike Worley, a very artistic and wunnerful guy, has publicly stated that he is going to start a weekly web comic! Wahoo! Huzzahs all around! Mike's art style is deceptive. It looks simple, even if it ain't. Here are some character designs for The Dibbles,.

Tell 'im Mark sent you.

(Best wishes in this endeavor, Mike.)

worleytoons.blogspot.com

An Obama administration, in the eyes of Focus on the Family Action
(2008-10-25 22:31)

The following is from the Christianity Today blog. I am impressed that the first few commenter's tore into the FoTF bilge. Their fear mongering and hateful way of going about their business disgusts me. As a Man of Faith, I feel I need to stand up and say that these Philistines do not represent me, my view of My Faith, nor my views of the Jesus Christ I know.

I don't know if I can urge you to read this drivel or not. I would suggest not, as it should only make you mad. Honestly, that's the only reasonable reaction I can see from somebody who has a shred of sense after they read more than the following clip. This really bothers me, as it appears quite obvious to me that this isn't based in Religious Fervor, but Fear. And an utter lack of faith.

My faith in G*d is strong enough to allow his will to be carried out. They seem to be making their G*d too small. Focus on the Family Action is the arm of this group that is legally separate from but a part of James Dobson's ministry. I don't care what good he's done in the past, this is beyond the bounds of what Christianity is all about. It makes me convinced that all Focus and related groups are interested in is Power. Nothing but Power.

Feh!

> clipped from [1]blog.christianitytoday.com
>
> **Focus on the Family Action posted a pretend letter in which a writer signed "A Christian from 2012" looks back on a Barack Obama administration in 2012, including terrorists attacks on four U.S. cities.**
>
> The letter proposes these scenarios:
> -The Supreme Court would lean liberal
> -Churches that refuse to perform same-sex marriages would lose their tax-exempt status
> -"under God" in the Pledge would be declared unconstitutional
> -Doctors and nurses who won't perform abortions will no longer be able to deliver babies
> -Pornography would be openly displayed on newsstands
> -Inner-city crime increases when gun ownership is restricted
> -Homeschooling would become restricted, so thousands of homeschooling parents emigrate to other countries such as Australia and New Zealand.

-"Since 2009, terrorist bombs have exploded in two large and two small U.S. cities, killing hundreds, and the entire country is fearful, for no place seems safe."

Sunday Sorrow (2008-10-26 17:26)

What had started out as a lovely Sunday, has turned sorrowful. Elaine's brother, Johnny, had a heart attack and died today. If you are so inclined, please keep her family, especially his young son, in your prayers...

Posted via LiveJournal.app.

Numb (2008-10-27 11:14)

Websters gives the definition of Numb as :

> 1 : devoid of sensation especially as a result of cold or anesthesia
> 2 : devoid of emotion : indifferent

Pretty solid notions of how I am feeling today. Except for the anesthesia part. None of that is needed today. A death in the family will do that to you without pharmacological help. Especially the death of someone you didn't like much.

Don't get me wrong, I wanted to like Johnny. I wanted to like him a lot. In his way, he was a good man. He took care of his family, was a tremendously hard worker, served his country with honor and was a lover of animals.

We didn't get along. I liked him well enough, but I know I am an acquired taste. Sort of like beer, I suppose. I have different views on many things, and it is hard to lump me into a pigeonhole. I wear my heart on my sleeve, my life has been an open book, I don't keep a lot of secrets and you really don't have to wonder about how I feel about you or anything else. Ask me, and I'm going to tell you. I may tell you even if you don't ask. I guess I'm a bit more like my mother in that respect than I care to admit most of the time.

Johnny didn't care for that level of openness, apparently. He got offended easily, yet never said anything about stuff until it all built up. Then it came out as a torrent of slights and hurt feelings. Most of them were fairly small to my way of thinking, and Elaine's as well. Yet, to him they were very, very real. Hence, a rift developed. Or worsened. I can be pretty clueless about reading other people and noticing clues.

What I do know is that since we moved out of a trailer on his land, I've only seen him once and that was at Tommy's funeral earlier this year. We hardly spoke then. Elaine tried to call him a few times, left messages and heard nothing back. Elaine swears up and down that Johnny changed before we got married. I don't know. I wasn't around so I can't say. What I do know is that he ignored Elaine's attempts to reconcile whatever was between them. That he wouldn't diminished my view of him as a man.

I don't know if I can ever quite forgive the pain he caused Elaine. But I know I have to, in order to be forgiven myself...

Just numb. That's what I feel right now. Numb and heavy....

A Fixed Mask (2008-10-28 11:36)

A Fixed Mask

Halloween
A torn rubber mask
Fixed with staples
A clown face with a slash
Hides a happy kid
My pillowcase doubles
As a treasure sack
Heavy with goodies
From the neighbors

Home I go to change
From a patch work clown
To a floppy hat
and Mother's wig
A different coat and
Out the door I go
To refill my treasure sack
Upon which I shall dream

...of another Halloween.

Writer's Block: Costumes (2008-10-31 08:33)

LJ Question: We have to ask: What are you going to be for Halloween this year? And can we see a picture?

I thought about dressing up as a Redneck McCain/Palin supporter.

My wife told me it was too scary for the cats...so, I'm wearing a generic costume. I look like somebody who cares. :-)

Two arrested after Obama effigy found on campus
(2008-10-31 11:23)

My only comments would be...that their momma's must be SO proud of them.

I was also disgusted to read that Sarah Palin was hung in effigy. What sort of loser thinks that this sort of behavior is acceptable?

I don't give a good gawd damn about your politics, just be responsible. And respectful.

> *clipped from www.cnn.com*
>
> **Two arrested after Obama effigy found on campus**
>
> (CNN) --Two men have been arrested in connection with an effigy of Sen. Barack Obama that was hung outside a building at the University of Kentucky in Lexington, police said Thursday.
> Joe Fischer, left, and Hunter Bush were arrested on disorderly conduct and other charges, police said.
>
> Authorities found a life-size effigy of the Democratic presidential candidate hanging from a tree outside the school's Mines and Minerals building on Wednesday morning, police said.
>
> Police said they arrested Joe Fischer, 22, a senior at the university, and Hunter Bush, 21, a former student at Bluegrass Community and Technical College.

More Right Wing Bilge (2008-10-31 20:16)

I got the following from somebody who knows I am not inclined to vote for McCain/Palin. Somebody who knows I don't appreciate getting this sort of crap in my inbox. I feel a strong need to rebut this piece of crap.

The following is attributed to Mark A. Gregg. Not a clue who he is....*my responses are in >italics*

Dear Mr. Obama,
It is August 30, 2008. My name is Mark Gregg. I am a 50 something conservative white male. I have followed your campaign closely, including the speeches you and others made at the democratic national convention. I am respectfully providing you with seven simple (probably shallow) reasons why I could never vote for you. I believe my opinion is shared by many people. While there may not be quite enough to prevent you from becoming president of this nation, I do think there is an awakening to the fact that you are not a (the) messiah that the media and liberal Hollywood entertainers are trying to portray you.

>>So far, so good....except for the Messiah bit...

1. I hear your mantra of change, change, change. Yet, you picked a long term, liberal, Washington insider (Joe Biden) to be your running mate. This is NOT change. It is a move that hypocritically refutes the very thing you supposedly stand for.

>>Actually, it was acknowledging that he (Obama) doesn't know as much as Foreign Policy as he thinks he needs to. He knows that Biden is a Foreign Policy expert and will offer competent and practical guidance in these matters. Not "front porch" appraisals of the "The Russians" that can be seen from there. Biden is well respected, and goes home every night. Talk about a Family Man.

Your campaign then slammed McCain for picking Sarah Palin, apparently, because she is NOT a Washington insider. She is a maverick who cleaned-up Alaska 's quagmire of political scandals. Which way is it, Barack? Is it okay for you to pick a Washington insider under the mantra of 'change', but not okay for John McCain to pick a smart, aggressive, reformer?

>>Palin's reforms obviously didn't include abusing her power as Governor. Not keeping her husband in check in his mad desire to get the brother in

law fired is a gross abuse of power. As she was found to be, then blithely says the opposite. Palin doesn't know the first thing about Foriegn Policy, Bush Policy, or Economic Fundamentals. The complaints weren't against her obvious outsider status, it was her obvious inability to do the job. Which she doesn't even clearly understand. Her anwers to questions about this have demonstrated that she's functionally clueless about basic Civics lessons.

2. You have the single most liberal voting record in the senate. This indicates to me and others like me that you may very well be an angry black man seeking to punish our country for sins of a different generation.

>>And you, Mr. Gregg, come across as a Racist. If you'd bothered to read his book, "Dreams From my Father," you'd know that he had already been down that path and realized it wasn't for him.

I am not racist. I have some biases just like you and every other human alive.

>> Saying you are not a racist doesn't make it so. And your accusation of "angry black man" is a racist statement, whether you choose to acknowledge that or not. It clearly shows your biases and viewpoints.

Unlike the democratic party who claims to be for the minority (but their record heavily refutes this),

>>Proof of this? Also, Democratic Party should be capitalized. It's a proper noun whether you agree with it or not.

I will give any person who truly needs help, help.

>>Who determines this?

I married a 'minority' girl 35 years ago (she is Hispanic) and have seen the evils of prejudice first hand.

>>Seeing it and being the recipient isn't the same thing. You may think you know, but you don't. I would no more try to say I understand the effects of being discriminated against than I would shoot myself in the foot.

However, I have also seen my wife and my children and others in her family throw off the veil of self imposed prejudicial bondage and move ahead.

>>Self-imposed bondage? What a condescending and foolish thing to say,

Sir. What was self-imposed about segregation? Being Red-Lined by lenders? Being viewed and treated as second class citizens? Having your own Grandmother tell you that she gets nervous around a group of young black men? When you yourself are black?

How ignorant can you be, Mr. Gregg? Are you truly this dense or this bigoted?

They love our country and do not view themselves any different than I view myself as a citizen of this country. Your lovely wife so disappointed people like me during this campaign when she stated it was the first time she had ever been proud of this country. She apparently never noticed the massive aid we give dozens of other countries. She apparently never noticed the sacrifice of literally millions of veterans who helped make this country a free nation and helped liberate other nations from brutal dictators such as Adolf Hitler.

>>Okay, you mentioned Hitler...the game is over....

>>Seriously, you didn't take her comments in context, did you? As a black woman, there is no doubt that she was pleased, surprised and proud that RACE was finally overcome, that a Black Man could be nominated to one of the two dominant political parties in this nation of ours.

>>Also, Laura Bush, the wife of the President who got us into this current disaster we're in right now, DEFENDED Michelle Obama. That ought to be enough for a Conservative White Male like you. A Republican said it, so it must be so.

She apparently does not remember that she attended ivy league universities with scholarship money that ultimately (at least some of it) was paid for by our taxes. This troubles me more than you know. She is an angry black woman who appears to not like her country very much. I don't want her representing me to the rest of the world.

>>There you go with the racist comments again. I doubt seriously that you would call Hilary Clinton a "Mad White Woman" would you? Why the "Black" in there? It's racist. Pure and simple. There ain't no two ways about it. Which says far more about you than it does about Michelle Obama.

3. You claim Christianity but apparently do not realize that the Bible teaches that he who does not work, does not eat.

>>Do you realize that this is actually the first principle of Socialism, according to Vladimir Lenin? No? I didn't think so...

Amazing how a Biblical truth can be perverted and used by all manner of people.

The Bible does not say or even suggest that he who CANNOT work, should not eat.

>>So, Mr. White Conservative 50-ish Male, what should the man who was laid off after holding the same job in the same factory for 28 years, because Managment (typically Conservative, White and Male) decide to move those jobs to another country because labor is cheaper?

>>Riddle Me THAT, Mr. Gregg.

>>BTW, do you remember the phrase, "Welfare Queen?" Because that's what your rhetoric sounds like you're railing against. We both know this is just White People Code for racism...

Yet, your liberal policies reward people who are capable of working, but choose to not do so.

>>Such as? You make accusations that are beyond general in scope, yet fail to provide specifics.

This bothers me. I know that if you are elected our taxes will spiral upwards.

>>At the risk of sounding snarky, I have to ask; "Are you a Seer or a Prophet?" You sound SO convinced of this.

You should heed the words of Winston Churchill: 'We contend that for a nation to try to tax itself into prosperity is like a man standing in a bucket and trying to lift himself up by the handle.' If I like anything about you, it is your campaign promise to balance the federal budget. Unfortunately, we have heard this a huge number of times from a number of different politicians and we realize that when you energize the very liberal Nancy Pelosi, Robert Byrd, Ted Kennedy, etc, etc, and the many other Democrats like them, a balanced budget will never, ever happen on your watch.

>>That's right. Just like it didn't happen under President Clinton. Oh...wait, excuse me...it wasn't just balanced...there was a HUGE SURPLUS. That the GOP pissed away whilst making the government multiple times larger in the process, got us involved in a useless war, avoided going after the true criminal in Afghanistan, and engaged in torture whilst dragging the good name of the USA through the World Mud...yeah, we need Four More Years of that...

4. During your question and answer session with Rick Warren of Saddleback Church your answer concerning the question of where does life begin, stunned me: 'Above your pay grade?'

>>*Yeah, I gotta agree. That was a stupid thing to say. Which he acknowledged a couple of days later.*

Does this mean when something bad happens as President of this nation that you are going to look at your salary to determine if you can respond?

>>*Heh! Almost clever...*

I am sorry, but this was the most serious gaffe I have seen you make.

>>*Well, then...everything else should be just great then. I mean, he did something that Bush never has done. He admitted he made a mistake and apologized for it.*

Frankly, it shows me that you are pandering in the most obvious manner. You will choose your words not from your heart, but from an agenda that I believe is still hidden from the American people.

>>*Again, you are getting into the realm of racist fear. What's hidden? Describe hidden? Where do you get these sort of ideas? What information are you basing these claims on?*

5. If anything stands out about you it is probably your appeasement mentality. In this era of rampant, radical Islamic extremism and with the latest stunt pulled by the re-energized Russian government, I am not sure appeasement is healthy.

I again revert to the words of Winston Churchill: 'An appeaser is one who feeds a crocodile, hoping it will eat him last.'

>>*Where did you get the idea that he (Obama) is an appeaser? Because he's willing to sit down and talk to people? That's nuts. To not talk, and hurl threats at each other is a surefire way to start fires, which cost dearly the lives of our young men and women. Thanks, I'll pass and let him talk to people. If that doesn't work, then we can knock the crap out of them. I'd just as soon end the days of the USA being the Big Bully on the Block.*

6. You and your party tacitly believe that a 13 or 14 year old girl must have the parents approval to have the school nurse provide them with a Tylenol when they have a headache at school. Yet, this same girl can become pregnant and the school can skirt her off to a clinic and abort the

child in her body without the parents knowing or being notified. This scares the hell out of me. You have two little girls. Would you be upset if this happened to them and you were not informed? Then why do you stand for this? It makes no sense to me.

>>Your answer presumes information not in evidence. Regarding Obama, I mean.

>>When is the Religious Right (which is hardly either) going to get behind educating people as to the best ways to prevent unwanted pregnancies? As Obama rightly said, nobody is FOR abortion, just the right to choose. It seems beyond illogical to me to be against abortion and likewise against practicing safe sex, and teaching our kids/young adults about it. Kids have been sneaking off into the bushes or barns for thousands of years. What makes you think not talking about it or "being against it" is going to change it now?

7. My seventh and final point (for now) is your supporters. I have watched the Hollywood entertainers that support you, systematically embrace Hugo Chavez of Venezuela and others like him.

>>Who has done this? Hollywood is a big place. Lots of people live and work there. How about some names, please?

I see the continuous smut and garbage produced by Hollywood, the very people who promote you the most vigorously.

>>Wait a second, My Friend. I am a White, Radical Moderate with slight Left Leanings, and I don't approve of smut. However, I'll be the first to fight for the right to produce and publish it. Your don't have to buy it. You don't even have to acknowledge it. And if you're bothered by the smut and garbage, why are you seeing it?

It is not a positive point to me and others like me to see these over-paid, bizarre, poor examples of human existence fawn over you and push you and your liberal agenda as hard as they do.

>>How do you feel about Muscle Man, Turned Actor, Turned Politician Arnold Schwarzenegger? And doesn't Matthew 7:2 apply here? (For with what judgment ye judge, ye shall be judged: and with what measure ye mete, it shall be measured to you again.)

The way I see it; When the devil is for you, we should question whether or not we should be against you.

>>Bwa Ha Ha! I got no other reaction for this...

In closing, I just want you to know that you scare me. I cannot vote for you. It is not because of your skin color.

>>To paraphrase Bill Shakespeare, "Methinks you doth protest too much" You have stated more than once that you aren't a racist. Let your words and actions speak for you, and not you for you.

It is because these items I've listed and many, many others like them. Do not claim that my dislike for you is race based. It is because I do not feel you have the best interests of this nation at heart.

>>When you constantly say you're not a racist, use racially charged phrases and expressions and say you're not a racist, it makes me think you're trying to convince yourself you're not a racist so you won't have any guilt about not voting for a Black Man. You don't like his policies? Fine. Got no complaint with that. Disagreeing (without being disagreeable) is what this great nation of ours is founded on. However, when you try to inject Race into the discussion, whilst claiming to not be a racist makes for a hard argument to swallow, never mind be taken seriously. You can't hide your racist spots, Sir. You've been undone by your own words.

Just a Reminder (2008-11-03 11:29)

Tomorrow is Election Day in the United States (Thanks be to G*D!) and all the hooey of the last two years will be over.

I care not a whit what your politics are. Tomorrow, it is your duty as a citizen to vote. To not do so is to diminish the sacrifice of those who died in defense of your rights and freedoms. Whether you agree with me, or don't...Go Vote!

Because, If You Don't Vote, Don't Bitch!

Condolences (2008-11-03 16:03)

I see that ABC news is reporting the Barack Obama's grandmother passed away.

Condolences to him, and his family at this time. With the election tomorrow, this leaves him little time to grieve.

Today (2008-11-04 08:06)

When we arrived at the polling place this morning, it was around 6:30. Reports on the radio had said there were lines, and a full parking lot at our local polling place, and while there were a lot of cars in the lot, when we got inside, there were only two people in line ahead of me. One of them being my lovely, patient and sainted wife, Elaine. G*d love her, she rode on the Gold Wing to go vote with me...

We have a choice to use the new-fangled, scary electronic voting gizmo's or good ol' fashioned paper and sharpie markers where you fill in the ovals. Elaine went Olde Skool, and I went to play with the new toy., We both voted, which is what is really important.

I'll be heading to Starbucks later this morning for free coffee, and am lamenting the lack of a Krispy Kreme in town, because a free star shaped doughnut sounds pretty good right about now.

Since the election is today, I'll be retiring politics from the roster of available topics for the foreseeable future.

If you haven't already, go vote. It's that important.

Some Final Thoughts (2008-11-04 22:19)

What happens next? Where do we go from here?

For Senator McCain, he still has a job in Washington.

Governor Palin still has her gig in Alaska, and probably has four words in her future. "Dancing With The Stars"

I hope that McCain's concession speech does some good and helps to heal some of the partisan wounds inflicted over the past 20 years. I doubt it, but it would be nice. That has to be my Pollyanna outlook on life...

I'm glad it's over, and congratulations to Senator's Obama and Biden.

Congratulations also to McCain and Palin. He showed true class in defeat.

The Morning After (2008-11-05 09:32)

I am pretty tired this morning. Staying up late watching election returns, and the wild celebration in Chicago last night. I'm plumb tuckered this morning.

So, I decided that listening to cheesy hair metal for a while this morning. I just hope it clears the cob-webs...if it doesn't work, then I may have to resort to the Partridge Family or something...

Writer's Block: Reading Aloud (2008-11-06 08:41)

LJ Question: **One of the highlights of going to a literary festival is hearing authors read from their own works. What author, living or dead, would you most like to hear read?**

Van Reid, hands down. His Moosepath League books are an absolute blast to read, and so flowing with brilliant prose that hearing him, with his Maine accent, read them aloud would be stupendous.

Sadly, his publisher has a severe case of HeadUpAssItis, and doesn't know how to publicize a book that got RAVES from the New York Times Book Review (a Notable Book, for the love of Mike!) because his books don't neatly fall into a particular genre. They're just good. Moron Book Publishers....the upside is that the books are cheap from places like Amazon.com and Alibris.com

Not that I'm bitter or anything...oh no! (My copies are all autographed!)

Reid's writing is somewhat reminiscent of Dickens, but it's far more accessible. There's whimsy, adventure, romance, farce, and memorable characters galore with such great names as twin Varius & Sundry Moss, and the beautiful ascenionist, Mrs. Roberto. I cannot recommend these books highly enough. Read the first chapter of Cordelia Underwood for yourself, and you'll see what all the fuss is about. Here's the link to the NY Times review of that same book.

So delve into the world of Maine, in the 1890's that Reid has so brilliantly created and lovingly written about. And when you do? Tell 'im Mark sent you.

——

A couple of other author's I'd love to hear read their work out loud would be Sir Arthur Conan Doyle. His creation, Sherlock Holmes became the bane of his existence at one point, so it would be grand to hear him read aloud something he didn't particularly like.

I'd also be interested in hearing Erle Stanley Gardner read one of his Perry Mason books aloud. And hearing Truman Capote read anything would be amusing.

http://www.nytimes.com/books/98/07/26/reviews/980726.26reedlt.html

Ok... It's Official! (2008-11-06 21:06)

I am officially sick of Xmas advertisements. And what's up with Xmas music all the time in Wally-World?

You heard it here 1st!

Posted via LiveJournal.app.

My Thanks (2008-11-11 08:18)

Today is Veterans Day, one of the days we set aside to honor those who have served this country. While the holiday was originally set aside to honor WWI veterans, it is now inclusive for all Veterans.

I will spend the day thinking of my family members who served, and I'd like to thank all those men and women who have also served that I might enjoy the Rights and the Responsibilities that go with them as a Citizen of this great country. It has its flaws, and I've no doubt that in the future they will be addressed and rectified. Still, it is the best thing going.

Thank you for your service. I am sincerely and truly appreciative. I salute you.

Writer's Block: Titular Heroes (2008-11-11 20:32)

LJ Question: Kurt Vonnegut's books have great titles, like Breakfast of Champions and Slaughterhouse Five. If your life was a novel, what would the title be?

"For Those Who Came in Late"

Because there was such a long period of time where there was much starting over...that or, "Lather, Rinse, Repeat"

Cat in the sink (2008-11-12 08:20)

Don't you just LOVE the 60's era pink sink with a cat in it? That's Poison Ivy in the sink. Pass the calamine, please.

I love the 1st Amendment (2008-11-12 09:32)

I really don't agree with what they are saying, but I certainly celebrate their Right to say it. And proclaim it. Even though I disagree, I also get to say that I don't agree. I also don't have the Right to be offended, and I'm sure that some Religious Zealots will be outraged over this...and consider it an attack on who knows what.

I shall pray for these lost souls.

clipped from www.cnn.com

The American Humanist Association unveiled the provocative $40,000 holiday ad campaign Tuesday.

WASHINGTON (AP) --You better watch out. There is a new combatant in the Christmas wars.

Ads proclaiming, "Why believe in a god? Just be good for goodness' sake," will appear on Washington buses starting next week and running through December.

The American Humanist Association unveiled the provocative $40,000 holiday ad campaign Tuesday.

In lifting lyrics from "Santa Claus is Coming to Town," the Washington-based group is wading into what has become a perennial debate over commercialism, religion in the public square and the meaning of Christmas.

"We are trying to reach our audience, and sometimes in order to reach an audience, everybody has to hear you," said
Group's new Christmas message: Be good, not godly

Silly things I remember (2008-11-14 12:52)

For no apparent reason, I remember that when my ex-wife (who I shall heretofore refer to as The Ex) was pregnant with our daughter, she craved ice water and ice cubes. Which was really strange, because before that, she didn't like her soda cold at all. Bothered her teeth a lot. Hormones mess with the body during pregnancy, I guess.

I remember bouncing off the walls when our little girl was born, and hollering, "It's a Girl! It's a Girl! It's a Girl!" like a mad loon telling everyone else what they already knew. I remember vividly cutting the cord, and making sure The Ex got to hold her first. She did the work...and I recall her laughing at my...exuberance in the aftermath with all the yelling. That's something I'll never experience again, sadly.

I remember when I was a small kid, and my mother quit smoking (it didn't take), she had this small frame with a cigarette butt glued to the middle of the page. It was supposed to be the last ciggy she ever smoked. When she started up again, I took it too her and just handed it to her. Didn't say a word. Pretty cheeky for a 9 year old kid. Speaking of which, I will have been a former smoker for 10 years later this month.

My sister's bedroom in our house in Minneapolis. She had the stairs to the attic in her room, along with a door and everything. Great place to hide, which she did. I also remember watching the tar on the roof of the porch bubble in the summertime heat. Later, making little balls out of the rubbery tar that the street department used to seal cracks in the road in our neighborhood in Ann Arbor.

I remember almost every step of my paper route, but not the names of the people I delivered the paper to. Isn't that strange? I remember much more of my days in Jr. High School than my High School days. Of course, I only went to one Jr. High and I attended 4 High Schools. Makes setting up accounts at Reunion.com and Classmates.com problematic.

I remember scratching my mother's back for a nickel for something like 15 minutes. Just think what that pile of coins would be with compounded interest today!

Just little bits and pieces of a lifetime.

Feeling old (2008-11-18 09:39)

I feel old this morning. I am now doing things my Dad does. Tilting my head farther back so I can see through my bifocals, for one thing. Having to adjust to new glasses far more often than before for another.

Worrying about things like cholesterol levels and watching my blood pressure.

And my joints are starting to ache when the weather changes...and I can't remember what else...

They say the memory is the first to go. I'll be damned if I can remember what goes after that...

Fleeting Clarity (2008-11-19 10:00)

Fresh and clear the nightmare woke him.
Like a stage, with the players on their marks
The image seared his mind, emblazoned for all time.

His own shout woke him up
Rattled out of slumber by his cry of fear
Or was he startled?

He'll never know for sure
For he'll ponder in the days ahead
What alarmed him so in his World of Dreams

That was once so clear
Before the light of day
Shattered the vision, like a broken mirror...

And caused the nightmare to flee,
   But the disquiet to linger.

Song of the City (2008-11-19 15:44)

The City sings.
   A constant song of
   Horns, and Busses, The
   Murmer of voices.

Vibrant and Alive;
   Familiar and always new.
   Children playing, street vendors,
   Air brakes sighing, and sirens.

The lurch and stop of the Subway
   Dirty doo wop singers
   Passing through the cars
   Chicken sack out for your money.

Illuminated by the Spectaculars
   The pulse of The City,
   Her decadence worn like a tiara
   For all the world to see
   Singing in his underwear.

The Chorus of the forgotten
   Trying to sell you a watch
   or a purse with almost
   the "right" name.

The Intro and the Coda
   Are the same.
   Over the rumble of a Jet plane
   The song remains the same
   And changes daily.

No Title (2008-11-20 08:22)

"Don't be a slut," he told her.
"Well....yeah," she rolled her eyes.
All he wanted was between her legs
He tried not to look at her rising and falling,
But he couldn't find her eyes.

Her name. (She has a name?)
He cannot remember. (Does he care?)
It doesn't matter, he tells himself.

"Don't be a slut," he tells her.
"Thanks, John. I'll try." Annoyed.
"My name is Mike!" Sucker punched.

"Whatever..." She walks away.

A Class Act retires (2008-11-20 10:37)

I am not a Yankees fan. Never have been. There have been some players of the Yankees I've admired over the years, and Mike Mussina is on that list.

We got the chance to see him pitch this summer at Yankee Stadium against his former team, the Baltimore Orioles. He got lit up like the town Christmas tree, but that doesn't change the fact that Moose was one of the best pitchers in the American League over the course of his career. 270 wins in this day and age should make him a lock for Cooperstown.

And he was a good guy besides. Best wishes to Mike in whatever he chooses to do next.

> clipped from sports.espn.go.com
>
> As expected, New York Yankees pitcher Mike Mussina has decided to retire, according to a baseball source with knowledge of the situation. Mussina informed the Yankees last week he would give them a decision by the end of this week.
>
> Mussina, who turns 40 next month, spent the last eight seasons with the Yankees after pitching for the Baltimore Orioles for the first 10 years of his career. His 270 wins rank second among all active right-handers, behind only Greg Maddux. In the final start of his career, he pitched six shutout innings against the Boston Red Sox to finish off the first 20-win season of his career.

Um…so…who cares? (2008-11-20 11:55)

Who really gives a rats ar$e about power babies? We have serious problems in this country and noting power babies shouldn't be one of them…

She's a cute kid and all, but let's get real. This is almost as annoying as Britney-Vision was a year or so ago…

clipped from news.yahoo.com

Suri Cruise tops list of Hollywood's power kids

LOS ANGELES (Reuters) "With her stylish outfits, stylish hair and stylish parents, two-year-old Suri Cruise has topped an annual list of the most influential celebrity children.
Suri, the regularly photographed daughter of actors Tom Cruise and Katie Holmes, toppled last year's winner Shiloh Jolie-Pitt to score top honors in Forbes.com's second annual list of "Hollywood's 10 Hottest Tots."

A Poetic Start (2008-11-24 12:58)

I'm kind of wondering if the thought is worth exploring. Your thoughts would be most welcome...

—--

Aiming a Digital Camera
   at Analog People
Converting reality to
   a plethora of
One's and Zero's.

——

I dunno...maybe this falls under the "Seemed Like a Good Idea at the Time" heading...

ARGH!! So irritated! (2008-11-24 13:06)

So, we were driving back from Columbus yesterday. Elaine was dozing in the passenger seat (much safer than dozing behind the wheel) and I was thinking about things to write about. And I hit upon the most fantastic idea. It was stellar. It practically wrote itself in my head.

I can't remember what it was about...

headdesk

sobs uncontrollably

Writer's Block: Eat, Drink, Be Merry (2008-11-25 08:25)

LJ Question: Thanksgiving is almost here in the U.S., heralding the start of the holiday season and the first of many meals where you might be confronted with a traditional dish that you happen to find disgusting. What holiday food do you hate to see on the table?

Oh that's so easy it's a gimme. I can't stand roasted turkey. Makes me feel like a communist to say, but there ya go.

It's pretty fowl...gimme a ham any day.

Recent Reads (Reviews) (2008-11-26 09:50)

His Excellency: George Washington by Joseph J. Ellis

We see him almost everyday. He's on the quarter, the dollar bill, Mount Rushmore and has the most famous phallic monument named after him. Somewhat appropriate the he was called the Father of Our Country with that in mind, don't you think?

But what do you really know about Washington, beyond the Parson Weems legend about the cherry tree. We all know that it's a legend and not true. We know he had wooden teeth. Or did he? What do any of us know about our First President?

This is the angle that Ellis brings to the table with this well written and researched biography. It's written in the more popular history/biography style that holds your interest. It gives enough facts that you get a real sense of the man and his times, but not so much that you fall asleep or skip pages. Or worse yet, put the book away before you've finished it.

Ellis' writing style is simple, almost lyrical in places. He has some notes at the back, but he keeps his audience in mind and keeps them to a minimum. This is an outstanding biography, and a great place to start to get to know the enigma that is George Washington. Washington, like all of us, was a complex man. He had his faults and foibles like all of us do. Ellis draws that out, puts some things in context and lets the reader make his own conclusions about others. He doesn't pass judgment. This book is highly recommended.

The Annotated Christmas Carol: A Christmas Carol in Prose by Charles Dickens (Michael Patrick Hearn, annotations, introduction)

I would be willing to be that while you know the story of The Christmas Carol from watching any number of film adaptations, that most haven't ever read the story that Dickens wrote in 1843. I am an unrepentant fan of Dickens. I've read several of his novels and enjoy them. I do tend to get a bit confused at times during the novels as some of the references are quite dated. This makes sense as these were mostly written during the Victorian Era (19th Century) and that was a heckuva long time ago.

That said, The Annotated Christmas Carol: A Christmas Carol in Prose is well worth reading. Hearn republishes his book from 1976 with more research materials available to him which brings so much more to the reader's enjoyment. Little entries about outdated words or word uses, common slang of the time is explained, and notes about possible locations used and sources for the scenes themselves as well as Dickens motivation behind them.

I found that even knowing the story so well, that I took great pleasure in reading Dickens words, his pacing, his sense of the time and of Scrooge. There are bits of Scrooge in all of the film adaptations, yet none capture him completely as Dickens wrote him. That's not a criticism, just an observation as film adaptations always differ in small ways from books. Different medium and all.

Even if you know the story forwards and backwards, it would behoove you to read Dickens tale as he originally invisioned it. Also included in the book is the Public Reading Copy Dickens employed in the last years of his life. That hasn't been available for over a century. Well worth the perusing in and of itself.

Thankful (2008-11-26 10:20)

- What am I thankful for this year? There are so many things. So many.
- My Savior
- My wife and best friend, Elaine
- My daughter, even though she is absent in our life
- Our family. That I was born with and that I have chosen
- Our Stoopid Cats (except the allergies part)
- LJ Friends, both new and old.
- My job
- Our home
- Our relative lack of debt
- Our relative good health
- The ending of the Bush Administration
- Beer
- Discovering Jazz

Just a few of the many things I have to be grateful for as we enter our Thanksgiving Holiday.

Wonder (2008-12-02 14:39)

I look at you
Wondering
What you think about.
Sitting there
So still and calm,
Your fingers flying,
The crochet hook a blur.
The yarn changes
To something else
As you sit quietly.
So, I wonder…
What you think about.

Time and Again -Memory Time (2008-12-03 11:16)

When I was a boy of 10, my Grandpa gave me a GE Clock Radio. AM band only, because in those days, FM really meant Forget Money. Nobody advertised on FM, nobody made money on FM and FM radios were pretty expensive at the time. At the time, all I had was an old Crystal Radio that I'd been given the year before by Grandpa. If you've never played with a Crystal set, you don't know what you're missing. It's a hoot to listen to radio that isn't driven by an external power source. Talk about Green!

So, as I was saying, I got this radio. At the time, we were living in Minneapolis, MN. Nice place, it was. I'd gotten attached to WCCO Radio, because that's what my Dad listened to. I didn't know there were other radio stations. They had baseball games, football games, hockey games, basketball games...all sorts of great stuff. And lo...there was this great program that was debuting called the CBS Radio Mystery Theater. Hosted by E.G. Marshall, under the direction of Hyman Brown. The Fear You Can Hear.

Yeah, it was all that and then some to a 10 year old kid. Some of those radio dramas really creeped me out as a kid. Scared the beejebus out of me. Made me lose sleep. One in particular stuck with me. It's haunted my dreams for years. This particular episode was called "Time and Again." About a clock with a 13 on the face. Ran on blood. Spooky stuff.
Since it's a sharing time of year, I share this particular episode with you. I hope the embedding of the show works. Just click to listen to the program. It's about an hour. For more fun and games, turn out the lights. Sit back, relax...and pleasant dreams!

(NOTE: The original post had the show available to stream)

Christmas CD's -Memories (2008-12-04 09:46)

I find it odd, that I can look at most CD's and not have a clue when I bought it, or where. Without fail, I can look at almost every single one of my Christmas music CD's and not only tell you when I bought it, but where and for how much.

There are a few Christmas CD's that are quite special to me. One is Phil Driscoll's Heaven and Nature Swing. Driscoll is a fine trumpet player and my Mother played trumpet when she was in High School. She was quite proud of the fact that she was the first girl to sit 1st Chair in the Trumpet section at her high school. So, when I first heard Driscoll's killer version of Joy to the World, I wasted no time going to Lemstone to buy a copy of this CD. Mother heard the trumpet part and had a look on her face that I didn't see very often. Rapture. She went on to say (after I played the song 3 more times) that it was apparent he was worshipping G*d with his trumpet. I can see (hear?) what she's saying.

Mother's gone now, so I tend to think of her a lot when listening to this particular song and album. It's also usually the first one I listen to when it's time for Christmas music. Further, it's also the song most likely to be listened to when it's not Christmas music time. It's that good.

Read Aloud (2008-12-04 15:30)

She returns from the mailbox,
Brushes the outside from her hair.
Closes the door, colored papers
Clutched in her hand.

"We got a letter!" She says.
Smiling, ""It's from Grandma!"
I wait, she removes her coat.

"Read it aloud, would you please?"
Carefully, she opens the letter.
Happy eyes dart down the page,
Laughter escaping before sharing.

I hear the voice of My Beloved
Read the words of My Dear One.
They deliciously merge, as their
Mingled words fill my heart.

After the letter is read
We put it away, in a box
Of treasured voices.
To enjoy. Another time.

Writer's Block: Untimely Passing (2008-12-08 11:40)

LJ Question: RIP John Lennon. The list of sudden and unexpected celebrity deaths is long—Princess Di, Heath Ledger, Kurt Cobain, Marilyn Monroe, and many more. Which one affected you the most on an emotional level?

I turned 17 the day John Lennon was killed. I was in the hospital at the time, and wasn't at all happy with life. Turning 17 was hard enough, as it seemed that my childhood was flowing away from me in a hurry. Then the sad news of Lennon's shooting breaks and I fell into a long period of depression.

So yeah...this one wins this dubious prize.

My Tools (2008-12-08 13:10)

In case you were at all interested, these are the tools I use to write. The notebook is a special edition Moleskinne made especially for Barnes & Noble, and the pen is a sterling silver Silver Eagle fountain pen.

I've been more prolific this year than in the past. I'm halfway through my 2nd notebook of the same size this year. It took me a couple of years to fill the last one.

Fiction. I understand the notion of telling the story, then clean it up later but I get almost pathological getting caught up in "writing" instead of "telling." Most annoying.

{no title} (2008-12-11 10:09)

The verdant brown
   of the snowless winter
Makes the cold seem worse.

The chill is sharper
   the wind bites deeper
Under the joyless skies.

The dun colored grass
   the bare naked trees
Everything cold exposed.

As the clouds sweep in
   driving the color away
Leaving a blanket of gray.

Or brown
   the verdant brown
Of the snowless winter.

Unknown Cool (2008-12-12 16:12)

I am so cool
   I may be too cool to
   Truly BE cool.

Dig?

The Cool Kids?
   They don't get my cool.
   They discount my cool.

Whatever.

The Uncool Kids?
   They don't get it either.
   So uncool, cool scares them.

Ain't no thing.

In my hip solitude
   My cool oozes
   Radiates its own cool heat

To the beat.

My cool is my own.
   You can't see it?
   Can't take it either.

Sucka.

My cool, it's unique.
   Like me, unlike you.
   There for no one to see.

So Lonely...

You can steal it,
   Fake it, not make it.
   My cool? It's my own.

Off the hook.

You see right through me
   You can't deny me.

I'm not gonna fade away.

Truth.

I got no bling out
   I got no need for it.
     My cool is apparent.

Ka-ching!

I am so cool,
   I may be too cool to
     Truly BE cool.

'S cool...

Writer's Block: Small Economies (2008-12-16 10:27)

LJ Question: The news is full of stories about people cutting back on their spending. What thrifty measures have you taken since the end of the economy as we know it?

We aren't eating cavier and prime rib these days.

Oh...waitaminnit...we didn't eat fish eggs and over priced beef before, so that's not helping.

We are eating at home more, and since my Green Bay Packers royally suck this year (Not Aaron's fault), I don't spend as much time or money of Packer stuff. And I've been buying my Jazz CD's used. Jazz music has become my latest obsession...

bet sheol (2008-12-16 19:23:48) hey, throw me a cd recommendation,

No Match (2008-12-17 14:01)

Inspired by a comment made by [fellow LiveJournal user]zenstone

No Match

The evil that men do
Shows how weak men can be.
They hide behind the lies
Of power; Fear their constant
Companion, ever at their side.

The evil that men do
Will never last, never win.
In the end, it cannot stand.
For the evil that men do
Is in no wise a match for prayer.

Writer's Block: Under the Same Sign (2008-12-18 10:05)

J Question: Today is chockfull of celebrity birthdays—Brad Pitt, Keith Richards, Christina Aguilera, and more. What celebrities do you share your birthday with? Do you find any similarities between you and those who share your birthday?

Um...Teri Hatcher and I share a birthday. So does Sinead O'Conner and the uber bitch of Right Wing Hate, Ann Coulter. I wonder if it's possible to petition for a new birthday? Also, Jim Morrison, Greg Allman, Warren Cuccurullo of Missing Persons (Great under-rated 80's band), Nick Nolte, Flip Wilson, Sammy Davis, Jr.,

The only similarities I can think of off the top of my head is that everyone puts their pants on one leg at a time.

Writer's Block: Now Showing (2008-12-19 09:09)

LJ Question: The holiday season is a big time for box office revenues. What Hollywood releases are you looking forward to seeing in the theater this month? What would you not go see even if someone paid you?

I'm not looking forward to seeing much of anything this year. There isn't enough money in the world to get me to see any movie with Will Ferrel in it.

Musical Memories (2008-12-19 15:53)

I've been on a real Jazz kick lately. I think I've mentioned that a time or twelve.

Anyhow, I took some time out from Coltrane to listen to Journey. I started with 'Escape' and went to 'Frontiers' from there. There are releases I've had on LP, Cassette, CD and Remastered CD over the years. Since nobody knows what the next big music format is, and I have too many CD's to even think about converting, I'm not worried...

I listened to these two albums (I've always had every release of theirs) a hell of a lot when I was a teenager and later. Many hours of these two albums in my car and volumes guaranteed to make my ears bleed. All without the benefit of sub woofers or anything like that. Just a solid little amp and some great 6x9's in the back dash...and it was blissful blasting.

But...and this is what really hit me today...I don't associate this music with people and events. I associate it with my car. Trips to Wisconsin, and driving to work and like that. I didn't really realize just how lonely I was when I was younger. How my nomadic lifestyle and the problems I created for myself kept me from setting down roots. Allowing me to make serious friends and commitments that I could keep.

I wanted to keep the commitments I made, just not enough to actually do what I needed to do. An inherent lazy streak that runs right through me like a runaway locomotive is something I fight like the devil every day of my life. I spent a lot of time worrying about how things 'should be' rather than facing how they were and doing something about it.

That changed before I met my wife. I've managed to repair of lot of relationships that I damaged or let suffer or caused to suffer during those years. There is only one that remains that is of tremendous importance. I live in hope I'll get the chance.

Anyhow, I just realized that this could a a huge part of the reason why I don't listen to Journey, Bob Seger or other artists I grew up loving and listening to for years. They actually remind me of a sad, lonely young man who disconnected himself with so much that life had to offer...and that I don't like to be reminded of those times.

Who knows...

Christmas Focus (2008-12-24 13:51)

Twinkling lights on the Christmas Tree
Glow brighter without my glasses
The soft focus of Christmas Past
   carries me away.

Lying on the living room floor
Or seated on the couch
My sister there beside me
Trolling through the brand new
Wish Book, from Sears & Roebuck.

Fingers tracing patterns on the
Slot car sets printed on those
Pages of wonder or dreaming
Of a bloodless war with
G.I. Joe and his Kung-Fu Grip
Or other fake devices.

Watching the news trains
Circle around the living room.
Sister's new doll house in
The center of the action

Looking at the tool sets
and pretty rings, wishing them
for Mom and Dad.
Another year when I gave Her pearls,
She gave me her heart.

We wondered how a Christmas Tree
Ended up in the Metal Detector wrapped for Dad.
One year there was a hair dryer
Under the tree, except it played records.

A little girl, snug in her tights
Pink dress, and bows in her hair
Falling sound asleep, on Christmas Morn
Her new doll clutched in tiny little arms.

The sounds of choirs singing
The malls so crowded
Strangers full of good cheer
Makes this a lovely time of year.

The twinkling lights grow sharper
I put my glasses back on as the pages
of my Christmas Past turn into
my Christmas Present

Writer's Block: Auld Lang Syne (2008-12-31 08:47)

LJ Question: For those who are into such things, this might be the biggest party night of the year. Other people like to keep it a little more low key. How do you plan to ring in the New Year?

I would love to help others ring in the New Year by making prank phone calls. However, another bit of childhood lunacy has gone by the way side with the widespread use of Caller I.D.

This truly saddens me. I well remember calling random numbers from the phone book and asking whoever answered if their refrigerator was running. When they answered in the affirmative, I'd holler that they should go catch it! Bwa Ha Ha....

Or how about this one? Call a drug store and ask them if they have Prince Albert in a can? You do? Better let him out, he's suffocating! Bwa Ha Ha!

Or this chestnut! Call the local bowling alley and ask the man who answers, Do you have ten pound balls? When he answers yes, ask incredulously, My God Man, How Do You Walk?

And a Happy New Year to you as well...

FWIW, I have about 20 empty Prince Albert tins. They are full of nails, screws and other useful bits of metal. I know this because there are labels on each and every one of them that tell me so. My Great-Grandfather did that.

Made in the USA
Charleston, SC
12 December 2009